How To Books

D0191991

Increase Your
Word Power

Increase Your Word Power

ANGELA BURT

How To Books

Published by How To Books Ltd, 3 Newtec Place,
Magdalen Road, Oxford OX4 1RE, United Kingdom.
Tel: (01865) 793806. Fax: (01865) 248780.
email: info@howtobooks.co.uk
www.howtobooks.co.uk

British Library Cataloguing in Publication Data
A catalogue record for this book is available from the British
Library.

Edited by Francesca Mitchell
Cover design by Shireen Nathoo Design
Cover image PhotoDisc

Produced for How To Books by Deer Park Productions
Typeset by PDQ Typesetting, Stoke-on-Trent, Staffs.
Printed and bound by Cromwell Press, Trowbridge, Wiltshire

NOTE: The material contained in this book is set out in good
faith for general guidance and no liability can be accepted
for loss or expense incurred as a result of relying in particular
circumstances on statements made in the book. Laws and
regulations are complex and liable to change, and readers
should check the current position with the relevant authorities
before making personal arrangements.

Contents

Introduction

This book has been written for students and general readers who love words and who would like to study them more closely in a structured way. It offers help and support to all those who are enthusiastic about extending the range of their vocabulary and who want to use words more precisely.

For example, Unit 7 will help you distinguish between 'perspicacity' and 'perspicuity' along with many other confusing pairs. Look at Unit 10 if you are sometimes at a loss when foreign words and phrases are used. You will be reassured to see the most popular ones listed alphabetically (and translated!).

Units 12, 13 and 14, among others, will help you see how many of our most difficult words have been derived. Once you understand the etymology, these words are demystified forever. For example, once you are familiar with the Greek root *khronos* (= time), then you have the key to the English words chronic, chronicle, chronological, chronometer, anachronism, synchronise and so on. And you are clear why a chronic illness is one that lasts a long time and is not necessarily serious. And in Unit 8, it's fun finding out who or what gave their names to the bikini, the fuchsia, nicotine, salmonella, sideburns and so on, and how the adjectives 'maudlin' and 'tawdry' have come down to us.

There are fourteen units. All but the first two introductory ones are arranged alphabetically for ease of reference. The book is very much a reference book as well as a practical self-help manual. 'Test Your Word Power' activities are included for useful and entertaining consolidation practice wherever appropriate and the answers to all the questions are given at the back of the book. There is, in addition, an appendix which covers the spelling rules for adding endings to words (useful when working through Unit 13). There is so much unnecessary anguish over spelling words like pin+ing, pine+ing, arrive+al, sincere+ly, budget+ing and forget+able. The rules are straightforward and the few exceptions are given.

You are advised to acquire a good dictionary if you haven't got one already to derive the fullest benefit from the activities. (See advice on choosing a dictionary in Unit 1.) A thesaurus is also a wise investment for anyone seriously interested in words. (See advice on buying a thesaurus in Unit 2.)

I very much hope that all who use this book will find it enjoyable as well as instructive and that it will whet your appetite for further exploration.

Angela Burt

Unit 1:
Dictionary Practice

It you are really serious about wanting to extend your vocabulary, you will need a good up-to-date dictionary that reflects current usage and includes recent additions to the language.

If you need to replace a dictionary, spend some time comparing different dictionaries in a good bookshop. See which one you are most comfortable with as you search for words. See which one gives the clearest definitions, with guidance about usage and information about the origin of the word. You may like to test several by looking up the same word in each of them, perhaps 'syllogism' or 'sesquipedalianism' or any other word of your choice!

▶ Regard the purchase of the best dictionary that you can afford as an investment. Have it to hand as you explore the units in this book. You will be ready to embark on a never-ending adventure with words.

▶ Use your dictionary to establish the meaning of the words in the following test. The answers are in the back of the book and you can keep your score. If your dictionary is adequate to your needs, you should score a total of 50/50.

▶ It would be unwise to work through subsequent units without replacing your dictionary if your score is significantly lower than full marks in this first unit.

TEST YOUR WORD POWER

Tick the one definition that you think comes closest to the meaning of each of the words on the left.

1. onerous   (a)   absolutely reliable   ☐
              (b)   burdensome   ☐
              (c)   single-minded   ☐

2. banal   (a)   poisonous   ☐
              (b)   commonplace   ☐
              (c)   impossible   ☐

3. feasible (a) practicable ☐
          (b) extravagant ☐
          (c) ridiculous ☐

4. surreptitious (a) illegal ☐
          (b) stealthy ☐
          (c) delicious ☐

5. iridescent (a) shining with all the colours
              of the rainbow ☐
          (b) pertaining to transport ☐
          (c) effective at thoroughly
              disinfecting surfaces ☐

6. cursory (a) rapid ☐
          (b) blasphemous ☐
          (c) curved ☐

7. perfunctory (a) fragrant ☐
          (b) superficial ☐
          (c) official ☐

8. plausible (a) elastic ☐
          (b) convincing ☐
          (c) playful ☐

9. rabid (a) doubting ☐
          (b) mad ☐
          (c) short-sighted ☐

10. trite (a) worthless ☐
          (b) neat ☐
          (c) hackneyed ☐

Match each word from the box with its definition.

accolade	inebriation
alliteration	inventory
autobiography	obituary
ecstasy	ostentation
histrionics	soliloquy

11. a list of articles, together with the
    description and quantity of each   _____

12. a person's life story which has been
    written by himself or herself   _____

13. a speech made by a character in a play
    when alone on the stage   _____

14. a showy display meant to impress   _____

15. a public tribute   _____

16. rapturous delight   _____

17. a brief account of a person's life printed
    on the occasion of his or her death   _____

18. the repetition of one letter or sound in
    a series of words   _____

19. state of drunkenness, intoxication   _____

20. exaggerated dramatic behaviour   _____

Use each of the words below in a separate sentence that shows you understand meaning and usage.

21. cynic

    _____

    _____

    _____

22. disinterested

    _____

    _____

23. allusion

    _____

    _____

    _____

24. ironical

_____

_____

_____

25. infer

_____

_____

_____

26. vehement

_____

_____

_____

27. aggravate

_____

_____

_____

28. literally

_____

_____

_____

29. sceptical

_____

_____

_____

30. conscientious

_____

_____

_____

Three of the words in each group of four below are closely related in meaning. Underline the odd one out.

31. despotic, eccentric, overbearing, tyrannical
32. irascible, cantankerous, diffident, choleric
33. denigrate, ruminate, cogitate, speculate

34. reprimand, admonish, castigate, exonerate

35. expensive, exotic, exorbitant, extortionate

36. rancour, asperity, aneurysm, acrimony

37. abrogate, arrogate, appropriate, usurp

38. bucolic, eclectic, rustic, pastoral

39. frustrate, foil, thwart, renege

40. garrulous, avaricious, loquacious, talkative

Match up the architectural terms in the box with the appropriate definitions.

architrave	eaves
bargeboard	gable
cornice	joists
dado	lintel
dormer	mullion

41. horizontal timber or stone above a door
or a window   _____

42. vertical triangular piece of wall at end of
ridged roof   _____

43. upright window set into a sloping roof _____

44. moulded frame around a door or
window   _____

45. timbers on which floorboards are laid   _____

46. wood along the edge of a gable   _____

47. vertical bar dividing the panes of a
window   _____

48. projecting lower edge of a roof   _____

49. horizontal decorative moulding along the
top of an internal wall   _____

50. lower part of an interior wall when of a
different texture or colour   _____

Score:_____ /50

Unit 2:
Thesaurus and Dictionary Practice

A thesaurus lists words similar in meaning to a given word (synonyms) and some thesauruses also list opposites (antonyms). Used in conjunction with a good dictionary, a thesaurus can be invaluable. It can prompt your memory when you can't think of the exact word you need or it can suggest an alternative when you want to avoid repetition.

Here is a typical entry.

> **look:** behold, contemplate, descry, discern, examine, eye, fix the eye on, gape, gaze, give attention to, glance, glimpse, goggle, inspect, leer, observe, ogle, peek, peep, peer, pry, regard, scan, scrutinise, see, sight, spy, squint, stare, study, survey, turn the eyes upon, view, watch

As you can see, a thesaurus doesn't distinguish between the shades of meaning of such related words. A dictionary will do this.

> **to glance:** to take a quick look
> **to glimpse:** to see momentarily or partially
> **to goggle:** to stare with the eyes wide open

If you don't have a thesaurus and want to buy one, spend some time looking at a range of them. Most are arranged alphabetically; the most famous, *Roget's Thesaurus*, is arranged thematically. Sample by looking up a word like 'look' or 'walk' in each of them. Choose the one you are most comfortable with. It's going to become a good friend.

'Thesaurus' comes from the Greek word *thesauros* meaning 'treasure house'. You will find a thesaurus can be just that.

Your thesaurus and your dictionary will help you with the following test.

TEST YOUR WORD POWER

Replace the underlined words below with five words or phrases that are close in meaning.

Kevin <u>threw</u> the brick with all his might at the window.

1. _____
2. _____
3. _____
4. _____
5. _____

It's a <u>fallacy</u> that everyone can learn to sing.

6. _____
7. _____
8. _____
9. _____
10. _____

Carmel was <u>delighted</u> at the birth of her first grandchild.

11. _____
12. _____
13. _____
14. _____
15. _____

Please give me an <u>honest</u> answer.

16. _____
17. _____
18. _____
19. _____
20. _____

The Minister's involvement in the <u>scandalous</u> affair is only now coming to light.

21. _____

22. _____

23. _____

24. _____

25. _____

With each group of words below, show how each word in the group has its own distinctive meaning and which common meaning all four words share.

26. gulp _____

27. pant _____

28. puff _____

29. wheeze _____

30. *common meaning:* _____

31. awe _____

32. esteem _____

33. homage _____

34. veneration _____

35. *common meaning:* _____

36. hilarious _____

37. ridiculous _____

38. uproarious _____

39. witty _____

40. *common meaning:* _____

41. irascible _____

42. irritable _____

43. morose   _____

44. splenetic   _____

45. *common meaning:*   _____

46. fee   _____

47. honorarium   _____

48. salary   _____

49. wage   _____

50. *common meaning:*   _____

Explain the difference between these pairs:

51. a band   _____

52. an orchestra   _____

53. a catalogue   _____

54. a programme   _____

55. a pie   _____

56. a tart   _____

57. a casserole   _____

58. a stew   _____

59. an apron   _____

60. a pinafore   _____

Give a synonym (a word similar in meaning) for each of the words below. The first letter is given in each case.

61. notorious   i_____

62. prohibit   f_____

63. ostentatious   s_____

64. clandestine   s_____

65. novice   b_____

66. stay   r_____

67. sleepy   s_____

68. abstain   r_____

69. intrepid   f_____

70. adhere   s_____

Choose words from the box which are most nearly the opposite of the ten words below it.

failure	enthusiastic
wealth	parsimonious
release	voracious
joy	occasional
retreat	permanent

71. generous   _____

72. abstemious   _____

73. temporary   _____

74. frequent   _____

75. apathetic   _____

76. advance   _____

77. grief   _____

78. success   _____

79. poverty   _____

80. capture   _____

Give the word most nearly opposite in meaning to each of these ten adjectives (describing words). The first letter has been given in each case.

81. prolix   s_____

82. vague   p_____

83. modest   b_____

84. rural   u_____

85. harmonious   d_____

86. voluntary   c_____

87. fertile   b_____

88. innocent   g_____

89. serious   f_____

90. synthetic   n_____

Match up the words in Column A with their opposites in Column B.
Draw a line to join them.

	A	B
91.	lethargic	lasting
92.	repellent	mature
93.	base	obscure
94.	heedless	automatic
95.	callow	unadulterated
96.	ephemeral	alluring
97.	renowned	wary
98.	naïve	energetic
99.	manual	sophisticated
100.	immaculate	filthy

Score:_____ /100

Unit 3:
People

WORDS DESCRIBING PEOPLE

There is a huge and wonderfully subtle range of words to draw upon when you want to choose a word to describe how someone looks, behaves or reacts.

Look closely at this alphabetical list, which includes nearly six hundred of them. Check the meaning of any unfamiliar words and be alert to exactly how they are used when you hear them spoken or see them written. In the course of time, you will make all of them your own and use them with confidence and accuracy.

abashed	abject	abrasive	abstemious
accommodating	accomplished	acerbic	acrimonious
acquiescent	adamant	adroit	affable
affluent	aggressive	aghast	agile
agog	alluring	aloof	altruistic
ambidextrous	amenable	amiable	amoral
amorous	anaemic	animated	anorexic
antagonistic	apathetic	apoplectic	apprehensive
ardent	arrogant	articulate	ascetic
assertive	assiduous	astute	audacious
august	austere	autocratic	authoritarian
authoritative	avaricious	avid	avuncular
barbaric	barbarous	bashful	bellicose
belligerent	benevolent	berserk	besotted
biassed	bigoted	bipartisan	blasé
blithe	blunt	bold	bombastic
boorish	bountiful	bourgeois	brash
brawny	brazen	brusque	bulimic
bumptious	burly	buxom	
cadaverous	callous	callow	candid
cantankerous	capricious	captious	cavalier
cavilling	celebrated	celibate	censorious
cerebral	charismatic	chary	chaste
chauvinistic	chivalrous	choleric	churlish
circumspect	coercive	combative	compassionate

compatible	complacent	complaisant	compliant
congenial	conscientious	conservative	constant
contrite	contumacious	convivial	corpulent
costive	covetous	crass	craven
credulous	crestfallen	crotchety	culpable
curt			

dapper	dastardly	debauched	debonair
decadent	deceased	decorous	defensive
deferential	deft	degenerate	dejected
demure	depraved	deranged	desolate
despondent	despotic	destitute	devious
didactic	diffident	dilatory	diligent
diplomatic	discerning	disconsolate	disgruntled
dishevelled	disingenuous	disinterested	dispassionate
dispirited	dissipated	dissolute	disreputable
distraught	docile	dogged	dogmatic
doleful	dominant	domineering	doughty
dour	downcast	downtrodden	droll
dynamic	dyslexic		

ebullient	eccentric	ecstatic	effete
effeminate	effusive	egregious	egocentric
egoistical	egotistical	elated	elegant
eligible	eloquent	emaciated	emasculated
eminent	empathic	enervated	enigmatic
enterprising	epicurean	equable	erudite
euphoric	evasive	exacting	exemplary
extroverted	exuberant		

facetious	facile	fallible	farouche
fastidious	famous	febrile	feckless
fervent	fervid	fickle	fiery
filial	flamboyant	flawless	flippant
fluent	foolhardy	forlorn	formidable
forthright	fractious	frail	fraternal
frenetic	frigid	frivolous	froward
frugal	frumpish		

garrulous	gauche	gaunt	gawky
genial	genteel	glib	gregarious
guileless	gullible		

haggard	haughty	headstrong	hedonistic

heedless	hidebound	hirsute	histrionic
hostile	hypercritical	hypocritical	hysterical
iconoclastic	idealistic	idiosyncratic	ignoble
ignominious	illegitimate	illiterate	illustrious
immodest	impassive	impecunious	imperturbable
implacable	importunate	impoverished	impotent
improvident	imprudent	inarticulate	incoherent
incompatible	inconstant	incorrigible	indefatigable
indifferent	indigenous	indigent	indolent
indomitable	indulgent	industrious	inebriated
inept	infamous	infantile	infantine
infirm	inflexible	ingenuous	ingratiating
inimitable	innovative	inscrutable	insolvent
insouciant	insubordinate	insular	intestate
intractable	intransigent	intrepid	introspective
introverted	inured	invincible	irascible
irate	irrepressible	itinerant	
jaded	jaundiced	jejune	jocose
jocular	jovial	jubilant	judgmental
judicious			
lachrymose	laconic	lackadaisical	languorous
lascivious	lax	lecherous	legitimate
lenient	lethargic	lewd	liberal
libidinous	licentious	lissom	literate
lithe	litigious	loquacious	lugubrious
machiavellian	magisterial	magnanimous	maladroit
malevolent	malicious	manic	manipulative
materialistic	maudlin	meek	melancholic
mendacious	mercenary	mercurial	meticulous
militant	misanthropic	misogynistic	moralistic
morbid	moronic	morose	munificent
myopic			
naïve	narcissistic	nefarious	negligent
neurasthenic	neurotic	nonchalant	nonplussed
notorious	nubile		
obdurate	obese	objective	oblivious
obnoxious	obsequious	obsessive	obstreperous
obtuse	officious	omnipotent	omniscient

opinionated overweening	opulent	orotund	otiose
pacific	pallid	paranoid	parsimonious
paternal	paternalistic	patriarchal	patrician
pedagogic	pedantic	peerless	peevish
pensive	penurious	peremptory	perfidious
peripatetic	personable	perspicacious	pert
pertinacious	perverse	pessimistic	petite
petulant	philanthropic	phlegmatic	placid
plaintive	platitudinous	plausible	plebeian
pliant	portly	pragmatic	precocious
prejudiced	prescient	presumptive	presumptuous
priggish	proactive	prodigal	proficient
profligate	prolific	promiscuous	prosaic
provocative	prudent	prudish	prurient
pubescent	puerile	punctilious	punctual
puny	pusillanimous		
quarrelsome quizzical	queasy	querulous	quixotic
raddled	raffish	rancorous	rapacious
rash	raucous	reactive	recalcitrant
reckless	reclusive	redoubtable	refractory
remorseful	remorseless	reprehensible	resilient
resolute	resourceful	reticent	ribald
rigid	rigorous	robust	rotund
rueful	ruthless		
sadistic	sagacious	sage	sallow
sanctimonious	sanguine	sapient	sarcastic
sardonic	saturnine	sceptical	scrupulous
scurrilous	sedate	seditious	sedulous
senile	sensual	sensuous	serene
servile	shiftless	shifty	shrewd
slapdash	slatternly	slender	slothful
sly	smug	soignée	solicitous
solvent	somnolent	sophisticated	spartan
splenetic	spruce	spry	squeamish
staid	stalwart	staunch	steadfast
sterling	stoical	stolid	strait-laced
suave	submissive	subservient	subversive

sullen	supercilious	surly	sybaritical
sycophantic			
taciturn	telepathic	tenacious	tendentious
testy	tetchy	thrifty	timorous
torpid	tractable	tranquil	tremulous
trenchant	truculent		
unabashed	unctuous	unkempt	urbane
uxorious			
vacuous	vainglorious	valiant	vapid
vehement	venerable	veracious	verbose
vigilant	vindictive	virile	vituperative
vivacious	vociferous	volatile	voluble
voluptuous	voracious	vulnerable	
waspish	wary	wayward	wilful
wily	wistful	woebegone	
xenophobic			
zealous			

TEST YOUR WORD POWER

Explain the difference in meaning between the words in these pairs:

1. authoritarian _____

2. authoritative _____

3. celibate _____

4. chaste _____

5. dominant _____

6. domineering _____

7. hypercritical _____

8. hypocritical _____

9. sensual _____

10. sensuous _____

Find the adjective in the box that best describes how each of these ten people looks.

brawny	gaunt
buxom	obese
cadaverous	petite
corpulent	rotund
emaciated	slender

11. Bridget is tall and *attractively thin*. _____

12. Matthew is *muscular and strong*. _____

13. Geoffrey's *pale, thin and corpse-like* appearance shocked everyone. _____

14. Danielle is undeniably *round and plump*._____

15. Helen is *daintily built*. _____

16. Brendan was *rendered thin and feeble* by his long illness. _____

17. Sheila is *large, plump and comely*. _____

18. Angela is *very fat indeed*. _____

19. Years of heavy drinking and lack of exercise have made Cyril *unpleasantly stout*. _____

20. Some people find Eric's *thin, lean and haggard* features very attractive. _____

Tick one definition which you think comes closest to the meaning of each of the words on the left.

21. splenetic (a) splendid ☐
               (b) athletic ☐
               (c) bad-tempered ☐

22. garrulous (a) talkative ☐
               (b) on the defensive ☐
               (c) over-confident ☐

23. hedonistic   (a)   generous ☐
              (b)   intelligent ☐
              (c)   pleasure-seeking ☐

24. supercilious   (a)   disdainful ☐
              (b)   very stupid ☐
              (c)   out-of-work ☐

25. cantankerous   (a)   competent ☐
              (b)   quarrelsome ☐
              (c)   vain ☐

26. zealous   (a)   with unreserved energy ☐
              (b)   with bitter envy ☐
              (c)   with deep regret ☐

27. droll   (a)   half-hearted ☐
              (b)   amusing in a wry way ☐
              (c)   kind and supportive ☐

28. ascetic   (a)   rigidly abstemious and self-denying ☐
              (b)   passionate about the arts ☐
              (c)   suffering from an advanced rheumatic condition ☐

29. meticulous   (a)   able to use either hand with ease ☐
              (b)   showing compassion ☐
              (c)   very precise about detail ☐

30. fallible   (a)   liable to make mistakes ☐
              (b)   sinful ☐
              (c)   untruthful ☐

Find in the box a word that is similar in meaning and a word which is opposite in meaning for each of the words below.

courteous	lazy
diligent	loyal
famous	notorious
frenetic	rude
inconstant	tranquil

	Similar	**Opposite**
serene	31._____	32._____
fickle	33._____	34._____
illustrious	35._____	36._____
surly	37._____	38._____
industrious	39._____	40._____

Choose the word from the box that best describes each of these people:

laconic	naïve
lethargic	phlegmatic
materialistic	sadistic
mercenary	sarcastic
misanthropic	sceptical

41.   Lynn is unemotional and not easily excited.

Lynn is.   _____

42.   Francis takes pleasure in watching others suffer.

Francis is   _____   .

43.   Blanche places a higher value on possessions and on worldly success than on spiritual values.

Blanche is   _____   .

44.   Jack is unwilling to believe what has been said despite all the salesman's efforts.

Jack is   _____   .

45.   Danielle is unsophisticated and trusting and doesn't understand how her actions may be misinterpreted.

Danielle is   _____

46.   Terry has a wonderfully terse way of expressing himself. He never wastes words.

Terry is   _____   .

47. Bruce has such a biting, hurtful, teasing way of talking to people.

    Bruce is _____ .

48. Pauline's motives are wholly actuated by the hope of making money.

    Pauline is _____ .

49. I'm afraid Georgina has no love for her fellow men and women and avoids them if she can.

    Georgina is_____ .

50. Phyllis lacks energy and drive. She seems half-asleep most of the time.

    Phyllis is _____ .

Check your answers with the answers at the back of the book.

Score:_____/50

Unit 4:
Occupations

We have a truly rich range of suffixes (word endings) to indicate job titles in English. The list below includes the most common ones with some examples. It is not exhaustive. You can add to it yourself from your own experience.

Notice that some of the suffixes sound notoriously similar and can present spelling difficulties:

▶ accountant and lieutenant but superintendent
▶ adviser but solicitor
▶ astronomer but ambassador

Notice too that some of the job titles included below are specifically male or female titles. Recent decades have witnessed a social revolution in the workplace, and assumptions about which jobs are suitable for men and which for women have had to be dramatically revised. Job titles like headmistress, usherette, masseuse, businessman, executrix and yachtswoman are becoming unacceptable to many. Such suffixes are asterisked to indicate that care needs to be taken. Neutral alternatives to gender-specific titles are examined in the next unit.

-ain (French)	captain, chaplain
-al (Latin)	admiral, cardinal, corporal, general, marshal
-an (Latin)	artisan, publican, sacristan
-ant (Latin)	accountant, adjutant, assistant, attendant, commandant, lieutenant, merchant, sergeant
-ary (Latin)	actuary, emissary, missionary, plenipotentiary, secretary, visionary
-ate (Latin)	advocate, curate, delegate, legate, magistrate
-ee (French)	bargee, employee, referee, trustee
-eer (French)	auctioneer, engineer, mountaineer, muleteer, pioneer, puppeteer, volunteer
-enne* (French)	comedienne

-ent (Latin)	agent, president, student, superintendent
-er (Anglo-Saxon)	adviser, archer, astrologer, astronomer, baker, barrister, biographer, boxer, butcher, carpenter, chandler, cleaner, draper, dressmaker, driver, farmer, geographer, grocer, hairdresser, indexer, labourer, lawyer, lecturer, lexicographer, manager, miner, minister, newscaster, officer, ostler, pawnbroker, philosopher, photographer, plasterer, plumber, porter, preacher, proofreader, reporter, stationer, stoker, teacher, trumpeter, waiter, writer
-ess* (French)	abbess, actress, authoress, conductress, deaconess, goddess, governess, heiress, manageress, poetess, prioress, prophetess, sculptress, seamstress, waitress
-et, -ete (Greek)	poet, prophet, athlete
-ette* (French)	majorette, suffragette, usherette
-eur (French)	coiffeur, entrepreneur, masseur
-euse* (French)	coiffeuse, masseuse
-ey (uncertain)	attorney, flunkey, jockey
-herd (Anglo-Saxon)	goatherd, shepherd, swineherd
-ian (Latin)	beautician, dietician, electrician, magician, mathematician, musician, optician, paediatrician, physician, politician, technician, comedian, historian, grammarian, librarian, parliamentarian, seminarian
-ic (French)	comic, critic, mechanic, mimic
-ice (Latin)	accomplice, apprentice, novice
-ier (French)	brigadier, cashier
-ist (Greek)	acupuncturist, archaeologist, archivist, artist, botanist, cartoonist, cellist, chemist, chiropodist, dentist, dramatist, guitarist, harpist, hypnotist, journalist, linguist, manicurist, motorist, novelist, numismatist, optometrist, orthodontist, philatelist, physicist, pianist, psychiatrist, receptionist,

	scientist, sociologist, typist, violinist
-ive (French)	detective, executive, representative
-lady* (Anglo-Saxon)	charlady, dinner lady, landlady, lollipop lady, tea lady
-lord* (Anglo-Saxon)	landlord, warlord
-maid* (Anglo-Saxon)	barmaid, chambermaid, milkmaid, parlourmaid
-man* (Anglo-Saxon)	businessman, cameraman, chairman, clergyman, craftsman, draughtsman, dustman, fireman, fisherman, foreman, frogman, houseman, layman, marksman, midshipman, milkman, ombudsman, ploughman, policeman, postman, salesman, serviceman, spokesman, stockman, workman
-master* (French)	choirmaster, headmaster, postmaster, quartermaster, questionmaster, quizmaster, ringmaster, stationmaster, toastmaster
-mistress* (French)	choirmistress, headmistress, postmistress, schoolmistress, wardrobe mistress
-monger (Anglo-Saxon)	costermonger, fishmonger, ironmonger
-on* (French)	archdeacon, canon, deacon, matron, patron, sexton, surgeon
-or (French)	actor, adjudicator, administrator, ambassador, author, chiropractor, conductor, councillor, counsellor, coordinator, director, doctor, editor, governor, instructor, juror, major, narrator, operator, rector, sailor, solicitor, supervisor, surveyor, tailor, tutor
-ot (Greek)	abbot, harlot, pilot
-path (Greek)	homeopath, osteopath
-smith (Anglo-Saxon)	blacksmith, goldsmith, silversmith, wordsmith
-trix* (Latin)	aviatrix, executrix, proprietrix, testatrix
-wife* (Anglo-Saxon)	fishwife, housewife, midwife

-woman* (Anglo-Saxon) chairwoman, charwoman, needlewoman, policewoman, servicewoman, spokeswoman, sportswoman, yachtswoman

-wright (Anglo-Saxon)   playwright, shipwright, wheelwright

-y (French)   deputy

-y (Scottish)   nanny

TEST YOUR WORD POWER

What is the specialist area of these experts?

1.   an apiarist   _____

2.   an orthodontist   _____

3.   an agronomist   _____

4.   a hagiographer   _____

5.   a forensic scientist   _____

6.   a paediatrician   _____

7.   a lexicographer   _____

8.   a psychiatrist   _____

9.   a taxidermist   _____

10.   a radiographer   _____

Complete the following sentences:

11.   Anthropology is the study of_____ .

12.   Biology is the study of_____ .

13.   Endocrinology is the study of_____ .

14.   Geology is the study of_____ .

15.   Horology is the study of_____ .

16.   Meteorology is the study of_____ .

17.   Oncology is the study of_____ .

18.   Ophthalmology is the study of_____ .

19.   Pathology is the study of_____ .

20. Sociology is the study of_____ .

21. Speleology is the study of_____ .

22. Theology is the study of_____ .

23. Toxicology is the study of_____ .

24. Zoology is the study of_____ .

What is the difference between the work of a councillor and a counsellor?

25. A councillor_____ .

26. A counsellor_____ .

What is the difference between the work of an astrologer and an astronomer?

27. An astrologer_____ .

28. An astronomer_____ .

What is the difference between the work of an entomologist and an etymologist?

29. An entomologist_____ .

30. An etymologist_____ .

Match the words in the box with the appropriate definition:

campanologist	mycologist
dermatologist	philologist
genealogist	psephologist
graphologist	seismologist
gynaecologist	trichologist

31. a specialist in women's ailments _____

32. a hair and scalp specialist _____

33. a fungi expert _____

34. a bellringer _____

35. a student of electoral and voting patterns _____

36. an expert on earthquakes _____

37. a handwriting expert _____

38. a family-history specialist _____

39. someone who makes a specialist study of the history and development of language _____

40. a skin specialist _____

Who would use these tools? Match each tool in the box with the appropriate user.

anvil	forceps
baton	gavel
chisel	metronome
cleaver	palette
float	theodolite

41. surveyor _____

42. musician _____

43. plasterer _____

44. artist _____

45. conductor _____

46. blacksmith _____

47. butcher _____

48. sculptor _____

49. auctioneer _____

50. surgeon _____

Score:_____/50

Unit 5:
Sexist and Non-sexist Language

JOB TITLES

The workplace has changed dramatically in the last 50 years now that women are taking their place alongside men, and the language of the workplace has had to reflect this change.

It is interesting to see how many job titles have been adapted or in other ways have been made inclusive.

Sometimes traditional male terms have themselves become neutral and are used for both men and women: an author nowadays can be a man or a woman, as can a comedian, a deacon or an ambassador. Sometimes it is traditional female titles that have become inclusive: both men and women can be nurses, nannies and au pairs. Sometimes an alternative title has been devised that will comfortably accommodate both sexes: firemen have become firefighters, stationmasters station managers and air hostesses flight attendants.

In the course of all this, some job titles have become necessarily redundant; we no longer have authoresses, poetesses, sculptresses, deaconesses, comediennes.... The list could be extended. Some titles, such as administratrix, executrix and testatrix, survive only in specialist contexts. Some '-ess' suffixes have survived. We have countess, baroness, princess; we have abbess and prioress; we have waitress and bus conductress. All these titles are perfectly acceptable although alternatives for waitress have been broached (waiton, waitperson) and there are fewer conductresses about in these days of single deckers. (Bus driver is a neutral job title.)

It may seem at first glance that conductor/conductress, manager/manageress and governor/governess are parallel male and female job titles today, but they are not. Although you will find both bus conductors and conductresses collecting fares on buses, you would find either a male or a female conductor conducting an orchestra. Although managers and manageresses continue to operate small businesses, both men and women would call themselves managers in larger concerns. The male equivalent of a governess is not a governor, and tutor and governor are both neutral terms today.

Mayoress and ambassadress have become ambiguous and need to be sorted. The wife of a mayor is a mayoress but technically a woman elected to a mayoral post can be called a mayoress too or a mayor. Similarly, the wife of an ambassador is an ambassadress but so is a woman appointed to an ambassadorship. She can be called an ambassador or an ambassadress and it is very confusing for everyone in this linguistic transition period.

And what of the suffix '-ette'? Traditionally, it has three functions: to denote the diminutive (kitchenette), to denote an inferior substitute (leatherette) and to denote the female gender. The suffix survives in drum majorette (by no means the equivalent of a drum major) and in usherette.

Both ushers and usherettes show people to their seats in cinemas and theatres (although usherettes are more in evidence) but the term 'usher' becomes neutral when men and women guide people to their seats in church, when they function as officers in courts of law, and when they perform ceremonial duties on grand occasions. Perhaps cinema usherettes will be called ushers too in due course.

Although 'male' and 'woman' can be attached to job titles when relevant ('May I see a woman doctor?'), avoid doing so unnecessarily. Male nurses are nurses and women engineers are engineers. Let us be grateful for neutral titles.

Gender-specific	Neutral
administratrix	administrator
authoress	author, writer, novelist, biographer, etc.
actress	actor
air hostess	flight attendant, cabin crew member
ambulance man	ambulance driver, ambulance worker, paramedic
barman/barmaid	bartender, barperson, barworker
benefactress	benefactor
binman	refuse collector
businessman/business woman	business person, executive
cameraman	camera operator, photographer
chairman/chairwoman	chair, chairperson
chambermaid	cleaner, hotel cleaner, room attendant
charlady/charwoman	cleaner, household helper

checkout girl	cashier, till operator
cleaning lady/woman	cleaner, office cleaner, household helper
clergyman	cleric, priest, vicar, member of the clergy
comedienne	comedian, comic entertainer
craftsman	craftsperson, craftworker, weaver, potter, joiner, etc.
deaconess	deacon
draughtsman	draughtsperson
dustman	refuse collector
editress	editor
fireman	firefighter
foreman/forewoman	supervisor
freshman	fresher
frogman	diver
gasman	gas board worker, meter reader
groundsman	gardener, caretaker, groundskeeper
headmaster/headmistress	head, head teacher, principal
heroine	hero, central character
instructress	instructor
insurance man	insurance collector, agent, representative
jury foreman	head juror
layman/laywoman	lay person, the laity (plural)
linesman	linesperson
lollipop lady	school crossing patrol officer
manageress	manager, managing director, MD
matron	chief nursing officer, principal officer, manager, superintendent
milkman	milk deliverer
patroness	patron
poetess	poet
policeman/policewoman	police officer
priestess	cleric, priest, vicar, member of the clergy

quartermaster	supplies officer, storeskeeper
questionmaster } quizmaster }	quiz show host
salesman/saleswoman	sales representative, counter assistant, shop assistant
schoolmaster/ schoolmistress	teacher, school teacher
sculptress	sculptor
seaman	mariner, sailor
signalman	signal operator
spaceman	astronaut
spokesman/ spokeswoman	spokesperson, representative, official
sportsman/sportswoman	sportsperson
statesman	statesperson
stationmaster	station manager
stewardess	flight attendant, cabin crew member
tradesman	trader, shopkeeper
wardress	warder
workman	worker, labourer

Idioms and expressions

It is possible to avoid exclusive language in many of our everyday idioms and expressions if we take a little care.

Here is a small sample of such expressions, and suggestions for rephrasing:

mankind	the human race, humankind
manpower	workforce, personnel
middleman	intermediary
sportsmanship	fair play
man-management	people-management
man and boy	from childhood
as one man	everyone together
man hours	working hours, work-hours

to a man	without exception
man-made	artificial, synthetic
the man in the street	the average person
odd man out	odd one out
man to man	person to person, face to face
be man enough	be brave enough
be your own man	act independently, be your own person
best man for the job	best person for the job
man's achievement	human achievement
to separate the men from the boys	to separate the experienced from the inexperienced
May the best man win.	May the best person/competitor win.
All men are equal.	Everyone is equal./All people are equal.
Time and tide wait for no man.	Time and tide wait for no one.
to man	to operate, to staff, to work, to run

Pronouns

Complications may arise later in a sentence even when a neutral job title has been used when it comes to pronouns and possessive adjectives. E.g. A doctor should aim to establish a trusting relationship with his patients. He can best do this by . . .

To avoid being gender specific (and it would seem quite inappropriate to talk about only male doctors in a general context like this) there are two possibilities:

▶ Include her (his/her patients) and she (he/she, (s)he).

E.g. A doctor should aim to establish a trusting relationship with his/her patients. He/she can best do this by . . .

▶ Make the advice plural by talking about doctors.

Doctors should aim to establish a trusting relationship with their patients. They can best do this by . . .

The plural solution is generally the easier one. Too many he/she, him/her, his/her references can be tiresome. These are all gender-specific; they, them and their are not!

31

Unit 6:
Animals, Birds and Insects

ANIMAL ADJECTIVES

There are some fascinating adjectives derived from the Latin and Greek words for many of our animals, birds and insects. All the words below are in current use. Some are used to describe humans as well: feline grace, asinine behaviour, an aquiline nose, etc.

anserine	of or resembling a goose; (of people) stupid (from Latin: *anser* – a goose)
apian	of or relating to bees (from Latin: *apis* – a bee)
aquiline	of or like an eagle; (of a person's nose) having the curved shape and pointed tip of an eagle's beak (from Latin: *aquila* – an eagle)
asinine	resembling an ass; (of person) obstinate, idiotic, stupid (from Latin: *asinus* – an ass)
bovine	of or relating to cattle; (of person) dull, stolid, stupid (from Latin: *bos, bovis* – ox)
canine	of or resembling a dog; (of human teeth) the four teeth pointed like a dog's (from Latin *canis* – a dog)
caprine	of or resembling a goat (from Latin: *caper* – a goat; odour of armpits)
cervine	resembling or relating to a deer (from Latin: *cervus* – a deer)
corvine	like a crow or raven (esp. colour) (from Latin: *corvus* – a raven)
elephantine	of or like an elephant; (of person) clumsy, large, awkward; (of memory) retentive (Latin from Greek)
equine	of or relating to horses (from Latin: *equus* – a horse)

feline	of, relating to or affecting cats; (of person) relating to grace and stealth, catlike (from Latin: *feles* – a cat)
hircine	of or like a goat; (of person) lascivious (from Latin: *hircus* – he-goat)
leonine	of or resembling a lion (from Latin: *leo, leonis* – a lion)
lupine	of, like or relating to a wolf or wolves (from Latin: *lupus* – a wolf)
ovine	of, relating to, or affecting sheep; (of person) sheeplike (from Latin: *ovis* – a sheep)
passerine	of or relating to birds with a perching habit (from Latin: *passer* – a sparrow)
pavonine	of or like a peacock (from Latin: *pavo, pavonis* – a peacock)
piscine	of or concerning fish (from Latin: *piscis* – a fish)
porcine	of, resembling, or affecting a pig or pigs (from Latin: *porcus* – a pig)
saurian	of or like a lizard; (of person) lizard-like (from Greek: *sauros* – a lizard)
simian	relating to, resembling, or affecting apes or monkeys (from Latin: *simia* – an ape, and possibly from Greek: *simos* – flat-nosed)
ursine	of, relating to, or resembling a bear or bears; (of person) bear-like (from Latin: *ursus* – a bear)
vermiform	resembling or having the shape of a worm (from Latin: *vermis* – a worm)
vulpine	of or relating to a fox or foxes; (of person) crafty, cunning, clever (from Latin: *vulpes* – a fox)
zebrine	like a zebra, striped like a zebra (etymology uncertain)

GROUP TERMS

There are some wonderful group terms for animals, birds and insects. Not all those below are in frequent use, but they are delightful in their own right, as well as being useful for quizzes.

antelope	a herd
apes	a shrewdness, troop
asses	a drove, herd, pace
badgers	a cete
bears	a sloth
bees	a hive, swarm
birds	a flock
bitterns	a siege
boar	a sounder
buffalo	a gang, herd, obstinacy
bullfinches	a bellowing
camels	a flock
caterpillars	an army
cats	a cluster, clowder (see also kittens)
cattle	a drove, herd
chamois	a herd
chickens	a brood, flock
choughs	a chattering
cod	a shoal
colts	a rag
coots	a covert
crows	a murder
cubs	a litter
deer	a herd
dogfish	a troop
dolphins	a pod, school
donkeys	a drove, herd, pace
doves	a flight

ducks	a brood (hatched as one family), a knob (small number of wild duck), a skein (in flight), a padding/paddling/raft (on water)
eagles	a convocation
eels	a swarm
eland	a herd
elephants	a herd
elk	a gang, herd
ferrets	a business
flies	a cloud, swarm
foxes	a skulk
frogs	an army, knot
gazelle	a herd
geese	a flock, gaggle, skein/wedge (in flight)
giraffe	a herd
gnats	a cloud, swarm
goats	a flock, herd, trip
goldfinches	a charm
goshawks	a flight
grouse	a brood, covey, pack
gulls	a colony
hares	a drove, trip
hawks	a cast
herons	a siege
herring	an army, school, shoal
hounds	a cry, pack
horses	a herd, stud, team (see also hunters and racehorses)
humming-birds	a charm
hunters	a string
huskies	a team
insects	a plague
jays	a band

jellyfish	a smack, smuck
kangaroos	a mob, troop
kittens	a kindle, litter
lapwings	a deceit
larks	a bevy, exaltation
leopard	a leap
lions	a flock, pride, troop
locusts	a plague, swarm
mackerel	a shoal
mallard	a flush
mice	a nest
minnows	a shoal
monkeys	a shrewdness, tribe, troop, wilderness
mules	a barren, rake
nightingales	a watch
oxen	a drove, herd, team, yoke
parrots	a flock, pandemonium
partridges	a covey
peacocks	a muster
perch	a shoal
pheasants	a brood, nye
pigeons	a flight, flock
piglets	a litter
pigs	a herd
pilchards	a shoal
plovers	a congregation, stand, wing
porpoises	a gam, herd, pod, school
pups	a litter
quail	a bevy, drift
rabbits	a nest
racehorses	a string
ravens	a crash, herd
roach	a shoal

rooks	a building, clamour, congregation, parliament
sea-lions	a pod
seals	a herd, a pod
sheep	a flock
skunks	a business
snipe	a walk, wisp
sparrows	a host
sperm-whales	a herd (see also whales)
starlings	a chattering, congregation, murmuration
sticklebacks	a shoal
stoats	a pack
storks	a mustering
swallows	a flight
swans	a bevy, herd, wedge (in flight)
swifts	a flock
swine	a sounder
terrapin	a bale
thrushes	a company
toads	an army, knot
tortoises	a bale
trout	a hover
turtles	a bale
walruses	a pod
wasps	a swarm
waterfowl	a bunch, knob
whales	a gam, pod, school (see also sperm whales)
whiting	a pod
widgeon	a knob, trip, bunch (on water), flight (in air)
wildebeest	a herd
wildfowl	a bunch, knob, plump, trip
wolves	a herd, pack, rout
woodcock	a fall

wrens	a herd
zebra	a herd

MALE, FEMALE AND YOUNG

There are some specialist terms for the male and female of the species and their young. It gives confidence to get them right.

creature	male	female	young
antelope	buck	doe	kid
ass/donkey	jackass	jenny	foal, colt (m) filly (f)
badger	boar	sow	cub
bear	boar	sow	cub
bird	–	–	nestling/fledgling
boar	boar	sow	piglet
buffalo	bull	cow	calf
camel	bull	cow	calf
cat	tomcat	queen	kitten
cattle	bull	cow	calf, heifer (f)
cod	–	–	codling
crab	cock	hen	zoea
deer	stag/buck	doe/hind	fawn/kid
dog	dog	bitch	pup
dolphin	bull	cow	calf
duck	drake	duck	duckling
eagle	eagle	eagle	eaglet
eel	–	–	elver
elephant	bull	cow	calf
ferret	hob	jill	kit
fowl	cock	hen	chick, cockerel (m) pullet (f)
fox	dog	vixen	cub, pup, whelp
frog	–	–	tadpole
giraffe	bull	cow	calf
goat	billy-goat, he-goat, buck	nanny-goat, she-goat, doe	kid
goose	gander	goose	gosling
guinea pig	boar	sow	–

hare	buck	doe	leveret
hawk	–	–	eyas
horse	stallion	mare	foal, colt (m), filly (f)
kangaroo	buck	doe	joey
hedgehog	boar	sow	–
leopard	leopard	leopardess	cub
lion	lion	lioness	cub, whelp
lobster	cock	hen	–
moose	bull	cow	calf
otter	–	–	pup
owl	owl	owl	owlet
peafowl	peacock	peahen	peachick
pheasant	cock	hen	chick
pig	boar, hog (castrated)	sow	piglet, porkling, gilt (f)
porpoise	bull	cow	calf
rabbit	buck	doe	kitten
rhinoceros	bull	cow	calf
salmon	cock	hen	parr
seal	bull	cow	cub, pup
sea lion	bull	cow	cub, pup
sheep	ram	ewe	lamb
swan	cob	pen	cygnet
tiger	tiger	tigress	cub, whelp
toad	–	–	tadpole
trout	–	–	fry
walrus	bull	cow	cub, pup
wasp	–	–	grub
whale	bull	cow	calf
wolf	dog	bitch, she-wolf	cub, pup, whelp
zebra	stallion	mare	foal, colt (m), filly (f)

ANIMAL HOMES

And lastly in this unit, let us look at the specialist terms for animal homes.

ants	formicarium (especially when artificially constructed for study purposes)

badgers	earth, sett
bears	den, lair
beavers	lodge
bees	apiary, hive
birds (captive)	aviary, cage
birds (wild)	nest
cows	byre, cowshed
dog	kennel
eagles	eyrie
fowls	coop
foxes	earth, lair
hares	form
horses	stable
lions	den, lair
mice	nest
otters	holt
penguins	rookery
pigs	sty
pigeons (domestic)	dovecot
rabbits (tame)	hutch
rabbits (wild)	burrow, warren
rooks	rookery
seals	rookery
sheep	fold, pen
squirrels	drey
tigers	lair
turtles	rookery
wasps	nest, vespiary

TEST YOUR WORD POWER

You may like to see how many of these questions you can answer from memory before looking up the answers.

Complete:

1. equine   like a_____
2. canine   like a_____
3. feline   like a_____
4. bovine   like a_____
5. aquiline   like an_____
6. _____   like a wolf
7. _____   like a bear
8. _____   like a fox
9. _____   like an ass
10. _____   like a lizard

Give the group terms:

11. a _____   of leopards
12. a _____   of eagles
13. a _____   of swans in flight
14. a _____   of goldfinches
15. a _____   of nightingales

Complete with the appropriate creature:

16. a barren of   _____
17. a sounder of   _____
18. an exaltation of   _____
19. a flush of   _____
20. a crash of   _____

Give the young of these creatures:

21. cod   _____

22. trout   _____

23. kangaroo   _____

24. zebra   _____

25. tiger   _____

Complete with the appropriate creature:

26. A parr is a young   _____ .

27. An elver is a young   _____ .

28. A leveret is a young   _____ .

29. A kid is a young   _____ .

30. A cygnet is a young   _____ .

Give the male of these creatures:

31. goose   _____

32. jenny   _____

33. mare   _____

34. duck   _____

35. doe   _____

Give the female of these creatures.

36. cob   _____

37. tomcat   _____

38. dog   _____

39. boar   _____

40. ram   _____

Complete this table:

	male	female
lobster	41._____	42._____
kangaroo	43._____	44._____
dolphin	45._____	46._____

Give the homes of these creatures:

47. hare   _____

48. beaver   _____

49. otter   _____

50. squirrel   _____

Score:_____/50

Unit 7:
Confusables

The hundred words in the list below are frequently misused. Take care! The list does not claim to be exhaustive.

acute   An ACUTE illness is a severe one of short duration.

chronic   A CHRONIC illness lasts for a very long time but is not necessarily severe.

aggravate   You AGGRAVATE a situation (= make it worse).

irritate   You IRRITATE a person (= annoy).

agnostic   An AGNOSTIC believes that it is not possible to know whether God exists or not.

atheist   An ATHEIST denies the possibility of the existence of God.

amoral   AMORAL means non-moral, without reference to a moral code.

immoral   IMMORAL means not-moral, not conforming to normal moral standards.

arbiter   ARBITER refers to someone with the power or the influence to set standards and make decisions (ARBITER of fashion, ARBITER of manners).

arbitrator   ARBITRATOR refers to an independent person officially appointed to settle a dispute between two parties. (Confusingly ARBITER can also be used in this sense.)

aural   An AURAL test involves careful listening.
oral   An ORAL test is a spoken one rather than a written one.

billion	Formerly British and American definitions were at variance:
	British: a million million
	        1 000 000 000 000
	American: a thousand million
	        1 000 000 000
	However, the American definition is now widely accepted internationally and in the UK. There remains, unfortunately, the possibility of being misunderstood and so care should be taken to remove any possible ambiguity.

million	In both American and British English, this is a thousand thousand: 1 000 000.
childish	CHILDISH means exhibiting or retaining the worst qualities of a child (immaturity, silly behaviour, petulance, etc.).
childlike	CHILDLIKE means exhibiting or retaining the best qualities of a child (candour, wonder, innocence, etc.).
complacent	A COMPLACENT person is smug and self-satisfied.
complaisant	A COMPLAISANT person is so anxious to please that he or she will eagerly fit in with the wishes of others.

complement/complementary

A COMPLEMENT completes.

▶ Well chosen accessories can COMPLEMENT an outfit.

▶ A ship's COMPLEMENT is the complete crew.

▶ COMPLEMENTARY medicine can complete the work of conventional medicine by dealing with areas beyond the scope of general practice.

compliment/complimentary

▶ A COMPLIMENT is an appreciative remark.

▶ COMPLIMENTARY tickets are given free of charge (with best wishes, as it were).

connoisseur — A CONNOISSEUR is an expert judge in matters of taste (from French 'to know').

dilettante — A DILETTANTE is a lover of the arts (from the Italian 'to delight') but with a suggestion of being an amateur dabbler, of not having studied the arts seriously or in depth.

contagious — A CONTAGIOUS disease is passed on by bodily contact.

infectious — An INFECTIOUS disease is transmitted by water or through the air.

continual — A CONTINUAL noise is one that stops and starts.

continuous — A CONTINUOUS noise is uninterrupted.

councillor — A COUNCILLOR is an elected member of a council.

counsellor — A COUNSELLOR is someone who gives advice professionally (a marriage COUNSELLOR or a debt COUNSELLOR, for example).

defective — A machine that is DEFECTIVE is not working properly. It has a defect.

deficient — A diet that is DEFICIENT in certain elements is lacking them.

dependant — A DEPENDANT is someone who depends on another for financial support.

dependent — If you are DEPENDENT on drugs, you

cannot do without them. There is no distinction in American English. The ending -ent is used for both forms.

discover

To DISCOVER something is to find it for the first time. It has, however, always been there.

invent

To INVENT something is to make something for the first time that has never existed before.

discreet

DISCREET means able to keep a secret, to be diplomatic, circumspect.

discrete

DISCRETE means separate, distinct.

disinterested

A DISINTERESTED person acts from unselfish motives. All personal interest is set aside (dis = away).

uninterested

Anyone who is UNINTERESTED is bored, not interested (un = not).

displace

To DISPLACE is to remove something from its correct place or to force someone from home and country.

misplace

To MISPLACE is to put something in the wrong place. MISPLACED affection is affection bestowed unwisely.

economic

ECONOMIC is derived from economics (the science of production, distribution and the structure of wealth). We can talk of the ECONOMIC health of a country or of an ECONOMIC rent (i.e. giving an adequate profit).

economical

ECONOMICAL comes from economy (the careful management of resources). A car can be ECONOMICAL on petrol or a meal can be ECONOMICAL (not wasteful or expensive).

egoist

An EGOIST is selfish and self-seeking as a matter of principle. EGOISM as a philosophical concept would encourage the pursuit of one's own interests as the highest goal, because the only thing one can be certain of is one's own existence.

egotist

An EGOTIST is selfish because he/she is too vain, self-obsessed, self-important or boastful to spare a thought for the needs or interests of others. All his/her attention is self-directed. An EGOTIST's conversation will be dominated by the use of I, me, my, myself.

enormity

ENORMITY refers to the quality of being extremely wicked, very evil. One can talk of the ENORMITY of child abuse.

enormousness

ENORMOUSNESS refers to the quality of being very large. One can substitute immensity, hugeness, bigness, vast extent.

▶ The ENORMOUSNESS of the task of cataloguing the neglected library is just beginning to be realised.

epigram

An EPIGRAM is a short, witty remark.

epitaph

An EPITAPH is an inscription on a tombstone.

equable

An EQUABLE climate is a moderate one without extremes of hot and cold.
A person with an EQUABLE temperament is even-tempered, calm and not easily aroused to anger.

equitable

EQUITABLE means just and fair. One can talk of an EQUITABLE division of wealth or labour.

exhausting

An EXHAUSTING task is a very tiring one.

exhaustive

EXHAUSTIVE means thorough, comprehensive. An EXHAUSTIVE

investigation would leave no stone unturned.

fewer FEWER means 'not so many': FEWER tomatoes, FEWER passengers, FEWER incidents.

less LESS means 'not so much': LESS sugar, LESS responsibility, LESS congestion.

fictional This means happening in fiction.

▶ Inspector Morse is a FICTIONAL detective.

▶ Middlemarch is a FICTIONAL town.

fictitious FICTITIOUS can be used like fictional to mean 'found in fiction'. It has another meaning also which has nothing to do with literature. It can mean false, not genuine.

▶ The child gave the police officer a FICTITIOUS name and address.

gourmand A GOURMAND loves food and frequently eats too much. You could say that a GOURMAND hugely enjoys eating and enjoys eating hugely.

gourmet A GOURMET is a connoisseur of good food and wine.

historic HISTORIC means likely to earn a place in history, memorable, significant: an HISTORIC meeting, an HISTORIC moment, an HISTORIC occasion.

historical HISTORICAL is used to refer to people who lived in the past and to events which really happened however insignificant.

▶ Robin Hood is an HISTORICAL character. (i.e. he really lived and is not fictional.)

N.B. Some events can be both HISTORIC (momentous) and HISTORICAL (they happened).

honorary	1. An HONORARY secretary of an association works voluntarily and is not paid.
	2. An HONORARY degree is conferred as an honour, without the usual academic requirements.
honourable	1. A decent HONOURABLE man is one with high principles.
	2. It is used as a courtesy title in certain contexts, for example, when referring to MPs within the House of Commons: the HON. Member for Plymouth South.
infer	To INFER something is to draw a conclusion from the evidence presented.
imply	To IMPLY is to insinuate, suggest or hint.
	▶ Are you IMPLYING that I'm a liar?
ingenious	An INGENIOUS device is one that is clever, inventive, original and suited to its purpose. Its originator could also be described as INGENIOUS and praised for his or her INGENUITY.
ingenuous	INGENUOUS describes a person (particularly a young woman) who is naïve and unsuspecting, frank, trusting and innocent. The remarks, smiles and aspirations of such a person could also be described as INGENUOUS. N.B. DISINGENUOUS means the opposite. A person who is being DISINGENUOUS is craftily pretending to understand less than is the case.
irony	IRONY is a gentle way of saying what you really mean by apparently stating the exact opposite. It comes from the Greek *eironeia* which means 'simulated ignorance'. An IRONIC remark simulates ignorance in order to amuse or to comment wryly on a

situation. A comment that a burnt lopsided cake 'looks delicious' is an IRONIC one.

sarcasm SARCASM may use an ironic approach but its intention is to wound and insult. It comes from the Greek *sarkazein* which means 'to tear flesh'. A SARCASTIC remark expresses scorn and contempt: 'I suppose you are proud of yourself, you loathsome, snivelling creature!'

judicial A JUDICIAL separation is one ordered by a court of law. JUDICIAL refers to the proceedings of a court of law.

judicious A JUDICIOUS decision is a wise one, showing good judgement. (One would hope that all JUDICIAL decisions are also JUDICIOUS.)

libel LIBEL is the defamation of someone's character or good standing in written form.

slander SLANDER is the defamation of someone's character or good standing in speech.

masterful MASTERFUL means powerful, authoritative, able to control others.

masterly MASTERLY means very skilful, as in 'a masterly performance'.

militate MILITATE comes from Latin *miles* (= a soldier). The word means to act powerfully (against), to be a strong factor in preventing.

▶ His frequent errors of judgement must surely MILITATE against his promotion.

mitigate MITIGATE comes from the Latin *mitis* (= mild) and means to moderate, to make less severe.

▶ The world may judge them harshly but there are mitigating circumstances.

observance	OBSERVANCE means compliance with the requirements of laws, rules and religious rituals. The word comes from 'to observe' in the sense of to obey, to follow, to keep.
observation	This means observing in the sense of watching, noticing and also commenting: OBSERVATION post; under OBSERVATION; a shrewd OBSERVATION.
perspicacity	If you praise someone's PERSPICACITY, you are praising their clearness of understanding, their perceptiveness. The word comes from the Latin *perspicax* (= seeing clearly).
perspicuity	If you praise someone's PERSPICUITY, you are praising their ability to express themselves clearly, their lucidity. The word comes from the Latin *perspicuus* (= transparent, clear).
psychiatry	The study and treatment of mental disorders.
psychology	The study of the human mind and its functions.
referee	An official who monitors play in certain sports such as football and boxing.
umpire	An official who monitors play in certain sports such as basketball, cricket and tennis.
reverend	This word means deserving reverence (a saintly and REVEREND man) and is a title given to clergy, usually abbreviated to Rev. or Revd.
reverent	This word means feeling and showing reverence: a REVERENT silence; a REVERENT genuflection.
sensual	SENSUAL means appealing to the body and its appetites (especially through food, sex and drink).

sensuous	SENSUOUS means appealing to the senses (especially through music, poetry and art).
sewage	SEWAGE is the waste products passing through sewers.
sewerage	SEWERAGE is the provision of drainage by sewers.
tortuous	A TORTUOUS path is one that is full of twist and turns. A TORTUOUS argument is similar convoluted.
torturous	TORTUROUS comes from 'torture' and means agonising, painful, involving suffering: a TORTUROUS fitness regime.
unexceptionable	This means inoffensive, not likely to cause objections or criticism.
unexceptional	This means ordinary, run-of-the-mill.
vacation	A VACATION is a holiday (from Latin *vacare* = to be unoccupied).
vocation	A VOCATION is a calling a strong feeling of being drawn to a particular career or way of life (from Latin *vocare* = to call).
veracious	A VERACIOUS person is truthful.
voracious	A VORACIOUS person has a huge appetite.
waive	To WAIVE one's rights is to forgo them, to refrain from insisting on them. WAIVE comes from the French word meaning 'to abandon'.
wave	To WAVE a hand is to move it backwards and forwards in greeting.

TEST YOUR WORD POWER

Select the appropriate word from the pair in brackets at the end of each sentence.

1. There will be a _____ basket of fruit and bottle of wine in your hotel room. (complementary/complimentary)

2. I was advised to apply for supplementary benefit for all eight _____ . (dependants/dependents)

3. My daughter was greatly helped by the study _____ at her school. (councillor/counsellor)

4. The librarian agreed to _____ the fine. (waive/wave)

5. Colin, as you know, is a _____ reader. (veracious/voracious)

6. Both parties eventually came to an _____ solution. (equable/equitable)

7. Gingivitis is highly _____ and so don't kiss your partner until it clears up. (contagious/infectious)

8. This list is not _____ but it contains the most common spelling errors. (exhausting/exhaustive)

9. I think you would find central heating more _____ than all these separate heat sources. (economic/economical)

10. Sarah had to get a taxi. She'd _____ her car keys and couldn't find them anywhere. (displaced/misplaced).

11. That diet is dangerous. It's _____ in all the basic minerals. (defective/deficient)

12. Percy Shaw _____ cats' eyes in 1934. (discovered/invented)

13. That's a very _____ bottle-opener you've got there. Don't some people have brilliant ideas? (ingenious/ingenuous)

14. In the country as a whole, _____ cars were sold last year. (fewer/less)

15. It was a _____ exposition of the causes of social deprivation – lucid, well-informed and objective. (masterful, masterly)

16. She _____ that I was thoroughly lazy although she didn't put it in so many words. (implied, inferred)

17. I can guarantee that Paul is totally _____ in all he does for the charity. He cares passionately about disadvantaged children. (disinterested/uninterested)

18. The Prime Minister considered suing the newspaper for _____ but then decided to ignore the attack on his

character in the editorial. (libel/slander)

19. Helen was kept in hospital overnight for _____.
    (observance/observation)

20. Moving to France was an _____ moment in the development of the firm. We've not looked back since. (historic/historical)

The words underlined below are not appropriate. Which words should be substituted?

21. The walls of the back kitchen were dripping with condescension. _____

22. You should really cook sausages very thoroughly to kill all the orgasms. _____

23. Beat the mixture until you get a good dropping constituency.

    _____

24. The students painted a colourful muriel on the nursery wall.

    _____

25. Mouth ulsters can be very painful._____

26. If you pull up on the grass virgin over there, you won't cause an obstruction._____

27. Amelia is not an easy child to deal with. She is very highly sprung. _____

28. After the educational psychologist's report, Nathan was given redeemable lessons twice a week. He's making real progress now. _____

29. The garden next door is terribly neglected and I suffer. There's convulsions growing all over the fence._____

30. If you're worried about little Jamie, ask your doctor to make an appointment for you with a paedophile._____

The words below have two different meanings depending on how they are pronounced.

e.g. Entrance (stress on first syllable) means 'a way in'.

▶ The main entrance is at the side of the building.

Entrance (stress on second syllable) means to 'fill with wonder and delight'.

▶ This production of *Swan Lake* will entrance all who see it.

Give the two meanings of these words according to which syllable is stressed.

31. present _____

32. present _____

33. reject _____

34. reject _____

35. invalid _____

36. invalid _____

37. converse _____

38. converse _____

39. project _____

40. project _____

Make clear the difference in meaning between each of the words in the pairs below.

41. confidant _____

42. confident _____

43. flaunt _____

44. flout _____

45. paramount _____

46. tantamount _____

47. ambiguous _____

48. ambivalent _____

49. bathos _____

50. pathos _____

Score:_____/50

Unit 8:
Eponyms

The English word 'eponym' comes from the Greek word *eponumos* (*epi* = upon + *onoma* = name). Oddly, and rather confusingly, 'eponym' refers both to the person after whom something is named and also to the name that has been formed in this way.

And so words like sandwich, lobelia and ohm are eponyms and so are the people whose names have been used, like the Fourth Earl of Sandwich, Matthias de Lobel and Georg Simon Ohm.

In the list of some interesting eponyms that follows, the derived names will come first and the people who have given their names will come second.

You will doubtless be able to add to this list with the help of a good dictionary that explains derivations. The study of eponyms is a fascinating one.

Achilles' heel	a weakness, an area of vulnerability In Greek mythology, Thetis, mother of Achilles, dipped him as a baby into the River Styx to make him immortal. However, the one weak spot was the heel by which she held him, which remained dry and unprotected. He was to be mortally wounded in the heel in the Siege of Troy.
Achilles' tendon	the fibrous cord that links the heelbone to the calf muscles This is named after Achilles. See entry above.
Adam's apple	the projection at the front of the neck (particularly visible in men) formed by the larynx. It is called the Adam's apple because traditionally it was believed to be where a piece of the forbidden apple had lodged in Adam's throat.

an Adonis

a very handsome young man
In Greek mythology, Adonis was renowned
for his great beauty.

an Amazon

a tall, strong, athletic woman
The Amazons were a legendary race of
female warriors, so named because they
removed their right breast to make drawing
a bow more comfortable. (Greek: *a* =
without + *mazos* = breast)

ampere

a unit of measurement of electric current
It takes its name from the French physicist,
mathematician and philosopher André-Marie
Ampère (1775–1836).

aphrodisiac

a substance that stimulates sexual desire
It is named after Aphrodite, Greek goddess
of sexual love, fertility and beauty.

assassin

a murderer of an important person for
political or religious reasons
The name comes from a fanatical Muslim
sect, active at the time of the Crusades,
called *hashshāshīn* (hashish eaters).

atlas

a book of maps
Atlas, the Greek giant condemned by Zeus
to hold the heavens on his shoulders,
featured on the title page of a C16th
collection of maps and gave his name to
such collections thereafter.

aubretia

a rockery plant
This was named in honour of the French
botanist Claude Aubriet (1668–1743).

August

When Augustus Caesar (63BC–14AD)
revised the Roman calendar by adding two
extra months at the beginning, he named
the former sixth month August after
himself.

Bailey bridge

a temporary bridge designed for rapid
assembly
Sir Donald Bailey (1901–1985) designed this
bridge. Widely used originally as a military

bridge, it is still used today in emergency situations.

balaclava
a woollen hat leaving only the face exposed
This head-covering takes its name from Balaclava in the Crimea and was worn by soldiers in the bitter winters of the Crimean War (1853–6).

bayonet
a stabbing blade that can be attached to a rifle
This weapon was first made in Bayonne, southwest France, from where it takes its name.

Beaufort scale
a scale for estimating wind speeds
This ingenious scale, depending on visual impressions, was devised in 1805 by Sir Francis Beaufort (1774–1857) when he was serving as hydrographer to the Royal Navy.

béchamel sauce
a flavoured white sauce
It is named after the Marquis Louis de Béchamel (d. 1703) who was steward to Louis XIV of France and devised it for him.

begonia
This beautiful plant was discovered by French amateur botanist Michel Bégon (1638–1710) on the island of Santo Domingo.

Belisha beacon
These were successfully introduced as a road safety measure by Leslie Hore-Belisha (1893–1957) when he was Minister of Transport.

Benedictine
A brandy-based liqueur, it was first made in a Benedictine monastery at Fécamp in northern France in around 1510.

bikini
This revolutionary and revealing two-piece swimsuit was so named after American atom-bomb trials on Bikini, an atoll in the Marshall Islands. It was considered that the effect of the swimsuit would be similarly explosive!

biro

(English tradename)
This famous ballpoint pen takes its name from its Hungarian inventor, László József Biró (1899–1985).

bloomers

Today this word is reserved for a voluminous and old-fashioned style of women's knickers.
When first devised by Mrs Amelia Jenks Bloomer (1818–1894) it was a revolutionary outfit, an entire costume consisting of tunic, short skirt and full Turkish trousers gathered at the ankle.

bobby

This affectionate nickname for a British policeman is derived from the Christian name of Sir Robert Peel (1788–1850) who founded the Metropolitan Police in 1829 when he was Home Secretary.
Seventeen years earlier, as Secretary of State for Ireland, he had founded the Irish Constabulary, members of which were nicknamed 'peelers'.

bougainvillea

This showy and very beautiful climbing plant was discovered in the Solomon Islands by French explorer and navigator Louis Antoine de Bougainville (1729–1811).

bourbon

The American whiskey distilled from maize and rye was first made in Bourbon County, Kentucky.

to bowdlerise

to remove from a text material considered offensive whatever the literary effect
Dr Thomas Bowdler (1754–1825) is notorious for having published his expurgated *Family Shakespeare* in 1818.

bowie knife

The weapon is named after Jim Bowie (1799–1836) but his father or older brother is generally credited with having invented it. Jim Bowie was a co-commander of the garrison which resisted the Mexican attack on the Alamo. He died in the siege.

to boycott to ostracise, to cease all social and commercial relations
Charles Cunningham Boycott (1832–1897), retired army captain and repressive land-agent in County Mayo, Ireland, gives his name to this extreme action. In an attempt to get the rents reduced, his tenants, encouraged by the Irish Land League, resorted to 'boycotting' him. They refused to pay the rents and blocked the delivery of all the supplies on which he was dependent.

boysenberry This hybrid of the loganberry, the raspberry and the blackberry was developed by American horticulturist Robert Boysen (d. 1950).

Braille The system of raised dots for reading and writing by the blind was developed by Louis Braille, who was blinded in an accident in his father's workshop at the age of three.

Bramley This cooking apple, possibly the result of bud mutation, was found growing in his garden by English butcher Matthew Bramley in about 1850.

buddleia The first specimens of this shrub were collected in South America by Scottish-born botanist Sir William Houston (1695–1733). At his request, the shrub was named after Essex rector and botanist Adam Buddle (c. 1660–1715).

bunsen burner This familiar small adjustable gas burner, widely used in laboratories, is named after German chemist Robert Wilhelm Eberhard Bunsen (1811–99).

Caesarian section a surgical operation for delivering a baby by cutting the wall of the mother's abdomen
This method of delivery is named after Julius Caesar, who is said to be the first person so delivered.

camellia	This plant, discovered by Moravian Jesuit missionary, Georg Josef Kamel (1661–1706), is named in his honour.
cardigan	knitted jacket with long sleeves, fastened by buttons This garment was first worn by soldiers in the Crimean War as a protection against the bitter cold. It takes its name from James Thomas Brudenell, Seventh Earl of Cardigan, who led the Charge of the Light Brigade in the war.
Celsius	a temperature scale by which water freezes at 0° and boils at 100° This scale, called Centigrade until 1948, is named after Swedish astronomer and scientist Anders Celsius (1701–44), who devised it in 1742.
cereal	This is named after Ceres, Roman goddess of agriculture.
champagne	This takes its name from Champagne, northeastern France, where it was first produced in 1700.
chauvinism	excessive attachment to a cause or country Nicolas Chauvin, a French soldier blindly loyal to Napoleon I, gives his name to this.
cognac	This term is properly reserved for brandy distilled only in Cognac, western France.
Colt	(trademark) This revolver was invented by American engineer Samuel Colt (1814–1862) and patented by him in 1836.
copper	Copper, one of the earliest metals to be used by humans, was in earlier times found chiefly in Cyprus, from which its name is derived.
currant	The name came into English from France, *raisins de Coraunt* (Corinth grapes).

dahlia	The plant was named in honour of the Swedish botanist Andreas Dahl (1751–1789) who died in the year it was discovered in Mexico by Alexander von Humboldt.
the Davis Cup	The international lawn-tennis championship for men is named after Dwight Filley Davis (1879–1945), the American statesman and doubles champion who instituted the competition in 1900 and donated the trophy.
Davy lamp	a safety lamp for miners It was invented in 1815 by Sir Humphry Davy (1778–1829).
decibel	a unit to measure the intensity of sound A decibel is 1/10 of a bel. Both decibel and bel are named after Sir Alexander Graham Bell (1847–1922), the Scottish-born American scientist famous for inventing the telephone and the gramophone.
denim	This material which originated in Nîmes, France, in the C17th was first called *serge de Nîmes*, hence denim.
derrick	This type of crane used especially for loading and unloading ships was named after its inventor, Goodman Derrick, a C17th hangman, who designed it as a gallows.
diesel	Rudolf Diesel (1858–1913), a French-born German mechanical engineer, invented the diesel engine in 1892, patented it in 1893 and exhibited the prototype in 1897.
Down's syndrome	This congenital disorder arising from a chromosome deficiency was first described in 1866 by an English physician, John L H Down (1828–96).
draconian	harsh, punitive Draco, a C7th BC Athenian legislator, is notorious for the severity of the laws he drew up in 621BC. Nearly every crime carried the death sentence!

duffel coat	The coat takes its name from the cloth, duffel, from which it is made. This woollen cloth with a thick nap was originally made in Duffel, Belgium.
dunce	a stupid person who is slow to learn Duns Scotus (c.1265–1308) was not stupid at all but actually a brilliant Franciscan philosopher. However, he and his followers (Dunsmen or Dunces) were ridiculed by C16th modernists as being unwilling to accept new theological ideas.
Electra complex	the unconscious sexual desire of a girl for her father, accompanied by jealous hostility towards her mother This is a female version of the Oedipus complex (see Oedipus complex). In Greek mythology, Electra, daughter of Agamemnon and Clytemnestra, persuaded her brother Orestes to avenge their father's murder by killing Clytemnestra and her lover, Aegisthus.
epicure	a person with discriminating taste in food and drink Epicurus (341–270BC), a Greek philosopher, taught that pleasure is the highest good. He did not advocate, however, excessive self-indulgence. He taught that mental pleasures were higher than physical ones and that moderation should be exercised in all things.
erotic	arousing sexual desire This is named after Eros, Greek god of love.
eschscholzia	(particularly well known is the yellow and orange Californian poppy) This honours the name of Russian-born German naturalist, botanist and traveller Johann Friedrich von Eschscholtz (1793–1834).

Fahrenheit	a scale of temperature measurement using 32° as the freezing point and 212° as the boiling point The inventor was Gabriel Daniel Fahrenheit (1686–1736).
Fallopian tubes	These are named after the Italian anatomist, Gabriello Fallopio (1523–62), who first described the pair of tubes in a woman along which the eggs travel from the ovaries to the uterus.
Ferris wheel	This giant fairground wheel with suspended passenger cars was invented by American engineer George Washington Gale Ferris (1859–96). The first one was huge and capable of carrying 1440 passengers.
filbert	This nut is named after St Philibert (d. 684) because it is ripe about the time his feast day falls (20 August).
forsythia	The Scottish botanist and horticulturist William Forsyth (1737–1804) is said to have introduced the shrub into Britain from China.
freesia	This delicate flower honours the German physician Friedrich Heinrich Theodor Freese (d. 1876).
Friday	Old English *Frigedaeg* – the day of Frigga Frigga, wife of Odin, is the Norse goddess of married love.
fuchsia	The shrub was so named by the French monk and botanist Charles Plumier in 1704 to honour the German botanist Leonhard Fuchs (1501–66).
Gallup poll	American statistician George Horace Gallup (1901–84) devised this method of sampling opinion.
to galvanise	to stimulate a sudden activity Luigi Galvani (1737–98) gives his name to this verb. He was an Italian physiologist, best known for his observation that in an electric field frogs' legs twitch.

gardenia	The flower was named in 1760 after the Scottish-American botanist Dr Alexander Garden (1730–91).
gargantuan	enormous, colossal (esp. of appetite) This is the name of the greedy giant in *Gargantua* written in 1534 by the French satirist François Rabelais (1494–1553).
gauze	This silky fragile fabric is believed to have originated in Gaza, Palestine.
Geiger counter	The device for measuring radioactivity was developed by the German physicist, Hans Wilhelm Geiger (1882–1945), with the help of German scientist, Walter H Müller (b. 1905).
to gerrymander	to redraw electoral boundaries to the advantage of one's own party The governor of Massachusetts, Elbridge Gerry (1744–1814), did just this in 1812. It was felt that the newly drawn boundaries looked like the outline of a salamander and the map was published in the *Boston Weekly Messenger* with the heading: 'The Gerry Mander'. He became Vice-President of the USA the following year!
Graves' disease	The Irish physician, Robert James Graves (1796–1853), first identified this disease of the thyroid gland which is accompanied by protrusion of the eyeballs.
greengage	Sir William Gage (1657–1727) introduced this variety of green plum to England from France in 1725.
to guillotine	The French physician Joseph-Ignace Guillotin (1738–1814) advocated this method of execution as being more humanitarian than by a sword.
guppy	The Trinidadian naturalist and clergyman Robert John Lechmere Guppy (1836–1916) sent a specimen of this freshwater fish to the British Museum in 1868 and it was named after him.

gypsy (gipsy)	Gypsies (or gipsies) were popularly supposed to have come from Egypt. It is now believed that they migrated from northwestern India in the C9th or so.
hamburger	Originally these were called 'hamburger steaks'. They originated in Hamburg, Germany.
herculean	showing superhuman strength and courage Hercules, son of Zeus and Alcmena, successfully completed 12 impossible tasks imposed on him as a punishment. After his death he was ranked as a god.
hertz (kilohertz)	This unit of frequency is named after the German physicist and pioneer of radio, Heinrich Rudolph Hertz (1857–94).
Hoover	(tradename) William Henry Hoover (1849–1932) recognised the potential of the electric floor-cleaner invented by J Murray Spangler, an Ohio department-store caretaker. He bought the patent in 1908 and set up a company to manufacture it. The company was renamed Hoover in 1910.
hyacinth	Hyacinth in Greek mythology was a very handsome youth, loved both by Apollo (god of the sun) and Zephyrus (god of the west wind). Hyacinth preferred Apollo and, as a result, was killed by Zephyrus in a jealous rage. The first hyacinth flower, it is said, sprang up from the blood of his fatal wound.
hygiene	Hygeia, Greek goddess of health, appropriately gives her name to this.
hypnotism	The name is derived from Hypnos, the name of the Greek god of sleep.
Jack Russell	The English clergyman, known as 'The Sporting Parson', John (Jack) Russell (1795–1883), developed this breed of short-legged terrier to work in foxhunts on Exmoor.

January	The name of the first month of the year comes from Janus, Roman god of doorways and passages. He is often depicted with two faces, one looking forward and one looking behind.
JCB	This mechanical excavator is named after **J**oseph **C**yril **B**amford (b. 1910), its manufacturer.
jeans	The word comes from the fabric from which jeans are made. 'Jean fustian' (fustian from Genoa) denoted in the C16th a heavy twilled cotton cloth.
jersey	The woollen worsted fabric was first made in Jersey, Channel Islands.
July	This month was named in honour of Julius Caesar after his death in 44BC.
June	The month was named after the Roman goddess, Juno, wife of Jupiter.
kaolin	The clay takes its name from the Chinese *gāoling* (lit. 'high hill'), the name of the mountain in Jiangxi Province where the clay is found.
leotard	a one-piece tightly fitting garment It was named after a famous French trapeze artist Jules Léotard (1842–1870). He died of smallpox at the early age of 28.
lesbian	The Greek poet Sappho in C6th BC wrote of love between women. She lived on Lesbos, an island off the coast of northwest Turkey.
Levi's	(tradename) Levi's are jeans manufactured by the Levi Strauss Company. Levi Strauss (1830–1902) was a German Jewish immigrant to the USA and a clothing merchant in San Francisco at the time of the goldrush. Using tent canvas he began making durable jeans in the 1850s for the Californian goldminers. He added rivets to the corners of the pockets for added strength.

listeria	a bacteria that attacks humans through contaminated food It is named after Joseph Lister (1827–1912), an English surgeon who took a particular interest in combating infection.
lobelia	This little bedding plant is named in honour of King James I's Flemish botanist, Matthias de Lobel (1538–1616).
loganberry	This hybrid of the raspberry and the American dewberry was first grown by the horticulturist, Judge James Harvey Logan (1841–1928), at his home in California in 1881.
to lynch	(of a group of people) to kill (someone) for an alleged offence without a proper trial Captain William Lynch gives his name to this distasteful practice. He was notorious for taking the law into his own hands and hanging people without trial in Virginia, USA.
macadam	See **tarmac**
mackintosh (macintosh)	Charles Macintosh (1776–1843) was the first to patent a lightweight waterproof rubberised cloth from which the first raincoats were made.
magnolia	This shrub with exotic creamy-pink blossoms is named after the French professor of botany at Montpellier University, Pierre Magnol (1638–1715).
marathon	The first unofficial marathon was run from Marathon to Athens in 490BC by a messenger who carried news of the Athenian victory over the Persians.
March	The third month of the year is named after the Roman god of war – Mars.
martin	This small European swallow is said to be named after St Martin of Tours because it migrates on or near his feast day (Martinmas, November 11).

masochism a mental disorder in which sexual pleasure is derived from the endurance of pain and humiliation
The Austrian novelist Leopold von Sacher-Masoch (1835–1895) described the condition.

maudlin tearfully sentimental (especially when drunk)
The adjective is derived from the name of Mary Magdalen, the weeping penitent in the Bible.

mausoleum a building housing a stately tomb
When King Mausolas of Caria died, his widow Artemisia had a tomb erected at Halicarnassus in his honour in 353BC. It was one of the Seven Wonders of the ancient world.

maverick an independently minded person who refuses to conform
Samuel Augustus Maverick (1803–1870) was a Texan engineer and rancher who refused to brand his calves.

Maxim gun the first fully automatic water-cooled machine gun
It was named after its US-born British inventor, Sir Hiram Stevens Maxim (1840–1916), who developed it in 1884. It was used extensively in World War I.

May The fifth month of the year is named after Maia, the Roman goddess of spring and fertility.

mayonnaise This thick creamy dressing was devised for the French Duc de Richelieu in 1756 to celebrate the capture from the English of Port Mahon, the capital of Minorca.

Melba toast thinly sliced toasted bread
It is named in honour of Dame Nellie Melba. See also **peach Melba**.

mentor	a wise and trusted adviser Mentor, in Homer's *Odyssey*, is adviser to the young Telemachus, son of Odysseus.
mercury	This heavy silvery metal is named after Mercury, the winged messenger of the gods, because it remains free-moving and liquid at normal temperatures.
to mesmerise	to transfix (someone), to command total attention The Austrian physicist Franz Anton Mesmer (1734–1815) discovered the power of hypnotism and so gives his name to this verb.
Messerschmidt	Messerschmidts were the standard fighter planes of the *Luftwaffe* during World War II and are named after Willy Messerschmidt (1898–1978). He had built his first aeroplane by the age of 18 and owned his first factory by the age of 25.
montbretia	This lovely orange and yellow member of the iris family is named after the French botanist, AFE Coquebert de Montbret (1780–1801).
Moonie	This is an informal term for a member of the Unification Church founded by the Korean industrialist Sun Myung Moon (b. 1920).
morphine (morphia)	Morphine is an analgesic and narcotic drug derived from opium. (Morphia is the old-fashioned name for it.) Appropriately, its name is taken from Morpheus, the Greek god of sleep.
Morse code	This famous code in which letters are represented by a system of long and short light (or sound) signals was devised by the American inventor Samuel Finley Breese Morse (1791–1872) who patented the system in 1854.

muslin	The fabric was first produced in Mosul, northern Iraq.
narcissism	excessive interest in oneself and one's own appearance Narcissus in Greek mythology spurned all offers of love, rejecting even the nymph, Echo. His punishment was to fall in love with his own reflection in the water of a fountain and to pine away.
nicotine	Jean Nicot (1530–1600) was French ambassador in Lisbon when Portuguese explorers brought back tobacco seed from newly discovered America. He introduced tobacco to France, in his turn, in 1560.
Nissen hut	The British engineer, Lt. Col. Peter Norman Nissen (1871–1930), designed these prefabricated arched corrugated iron shelters used extensively in both World Wars and still surviving in many civilian situations today.
Nobel prize	Alfred Bernhard Nobel (1833–96) invented dynamite (1866), gelignite and other high explosives. The Swedish chemist, engineer and manufacturer was a pacifist. He hoped that his invention would help preserve peace. He endowed six prizes to be awarded annually (for physics, chemistry, medicine, literature, economics and peace). The first prizes were awarded in 1901.
Oedipus complex	the unconscious sexual attraction of a child (especially a boy) to the parent of the opposite sex In Greek mythology, Oedipus, the son of Laius and Jocasta, the king and queen of Thebes, was left to die on a mountain top as a baby when his father learned from the oracle that he would die at the hand of his son. The baby Oedipus was rescued by a shepherd. Later, unaware of his true identity, he killed Laius and married his

mother Jocasta, by whom he had four children. When he discovered his parentage, he tore out his eyes, and Jocasta committed suicide.

ohm

A metric unit of electrical resistance, it is named after the German physicist, Georg Simon Ohm (1787–1854).

Oscar

a nickname for the gold statuette first awarded by the Academy of Motion Picture Arts and Sciences in 1928
It is claimed that the nickname was born when Margaret Herrick, the Academy librarian, said that the statuette reminded her of her Uncle Oscar (Oscar Pierce, a wheat and fruit grower).

Pap test

a cervical smear test that is carried out to detect uterine cancer
The test was devised by Greek-born American anatomist, George Nicholas Papanicolaou (1883–1962).

Parkinson's disease

It is named after the English surgeon James Parkinson (1755–1824) who first described it in 1817.

to pasteurise

to destroy bacteria in milk and other substances by heating
This process is named after the French chemist and bacteriologist Louis Pasteur (1822–95) who first devised it.

pavlova

a dessert of meringue topped with fruit and cream
This delicious concoction was devised by Australian chefs to honour the ballerina, Anna Pavlova (1884–1931), during a tour of Australia and New Zealand.

peach Melba

a dessert of peaches, ice cream and raspberry melba sauce
French chef, Auguste Escoffier (1846–1935), devised this dessert to honour Dame Nellie Melba, the Australian opera singer (1861–1931).

Plimsoll line	the lines on the sides of ships which indicate safe loading levels Samuel Plimsoll (1824–98), MP for Derby, was a leading proponent of shipping reform. He helped to bring in the Merchant Shipping Act of 1876 which ended the practice of sending overloaded ships to sea. (The rubber-soled canvas shoes are said to be called plimsolls because the top edge of the rubber resembles a plimsoll line!)
poinsettia	The American diplomat and amateur botanist, Joel Roberts Pointsett (1779–1851), sent back specimens of the plant to the USA when he was American Ambassador to Mexico in 1825. It was named after him even though it had been introduced previously.
procrustean	that which produces uniformity by arbitrary or violent means Procrustes was a particularly unpleasant Athenian who tied his victims to a bed. If they were too short to reach the end of it, he stretched them; if they were too long, he chopped off the ends of their legs.
Pullman car	a comfortable, luxurious railway carriage with waiter service The American inventor, George Mortimer Pullman (1831–1897), designed these carriages.
Pyrrhic victory	a victory won at such a cost that it is no victory at all King Pyrrhus of Epirus (c307–272BC) won a series of victories sustaining heavy losses against Rome, particularly at Asculum (279BC). He is reported to have said that he couldn't afford any more victories like that.
quisling	a traitor Major Vidkun Abraham Quisling (1887–1945), a Norwegian politician, collaborated with the Germans and helped them invade

his country in World War II. He ruled Norway on behalf of the German occupying forces (1940–45). After the war, he was found guilty of war crimes and shot.

quixotic
unrealistically and impractically idealistic
Don Quixote in the novel by Miguel de Cervantes Saavedra exemplifies this adjective.

raglan sleeves
sleeves set in from the neck edge to the armpit, so avoiding the need for a shoulder seam
Lord Raglan (1788–1855), a British commander of the Crimean War (1853–6) wore a coat with such sleeves. He had been wounded at the Battle of Waterloo (1815) and had had his left arm amputated. This style of sleeve would have been easier for him to wear.

Richter scale
a scale for measuring the intensity of earthquakes
This is sometimes known as the Gutenberg-Richter scale. American seismologist, Charles F Richter (1900–1985), devised the scale in 1935 in association with the German Bruno Gutenberg (1889–1960).

Rolls-Royce
Such is the veneration in which the luxury cars are held that the term Rolls-Royce has come to indicate quality itself.
The Hon. Charles Stewart Rolls (1877–1910), motoring and aviation pioneer (he made the first double crossing of the English Channel shortly before he was killed in a flying accident), and Sir Frederick Henry Royce (1863–1933) formed the company Rolls-Royce in 1906.

a Romeo
a passionate young male lover
Romeo's name (*Romeo and Juliet* by William Shakespeare) has been thus perpetuated.

Rubik's cube
a puzzle cube
Its Hungarian inventor, Erno Rubik

(b. 1944), devised it to help his students understand three-dimensional design. It became a craze after being shown at a mathematics conference in 1978.

rudbeckia
This plant is named after the Swedish botanist, Olaf Rudbek (1660–1740).

rugby
The game was first played at Rugby School, the English public school.

sadism
a perversion by which sexual satisfaction is enjoyed while inflicting pain on others
Donatien Alphonse François, Marquis de Sade (1740–1814), a French cavalry officer notorious for cruelty and debauchery, wrote works describing such behaviour while in prison.

salmonella
a bacterium that causes food poisoning
The American veterinary surgeon, David Elmer Salmon (1850–1914), after whom it is named, was the first to identify it.

sandwich
This is famously named after John Montague, the Fourth Earl of Sandwich (1718–1792), who was addicted to gambling. He preferred to eat without leaving the gaming tables and his valet would bring him meat between two slices of bread.

Sanforised
(trademark) pre-shrunk
Sanford Lockwood Cluett (1874–1968), the American director of engineering research at a firm of shirt and collar manufacturers, invented this process of pre-shrinking cotton.

Saturday
This day of the week is named after Saturn, the Roman god of agriculture.

saxophone
This musical instrument was invented by Antoine-Joseph (Adolphe) Sax (1814–1894), a Belgian instrument-maker. It was first shown in public in 1844.

a Scrooge
an excessively mean and cheerless person
Ebenezer Scrooge in *A Christmas Carol* by

Charles Dickens (first published in book form in 1861) has been identified with all such miserly killjoys.

a Shylock   Shylock in William Shakespeare's *The Merchant of Venice* (c. 1596) has been identified with all moneylenders who charge exorbitant rates of interest.

sideburns   sidewhiskers worn with a clean-shaven chin American-Civil-War General Ambrose Everett Burnside (1824–81) popularised this hairy style. Why they are called sideburns and not burnsides is not known!

silhouette   in portraiture just the outlined likeness cut from dark material and mounted on a light background
The French politician, Etienne de Silhouette (1709–1767), has lent his name to this portrait style but one can only speculate why. One suggestion is that his notorious meanness led him to favour unfinished portraits (which would cost less).

spoonerisms   The Rev. William Archibald Spooner (1844–1930) is famous for apparently accidental verbal transpositions whereby a 'half-formed wish' comes out as a 'half-wormed fish' and 'Conquering Kings' becomes 'Kinquering Kongs'. There are many other examples which are well worth collecting.

Stetson   (trademark)
This broad-brimmed cowboy hat was designed by American hat-manufacturer, John Batterson Stetson (1830–1906).

tangerine   This fruit exported from Tangier, on the northern coast of Morocco, was originally called 'the tangerine orange'.

to tantalise   to torment or tease someone with the sight or promise of something that is then withdrawn
Tantalus, the mythical king of Phrygia, was

'tantalised' by the gods for offences against them. He was made to stand in water that receded when he tried to drink it beneath fruit trees whose branches moved away whenever he tried to pick the fruit.

tarmac
(UK tradename)
John Loudon McAdam (1756–1836), a British surveyor, pioneered a system of road-surfacing using layers of compacted broken stone bound with bitumen or tar. The Tarmacadam Company of which tarmac is an abbreviation was formed in 1903.

tawdry
showy but cheap; poor quality
Tawdry is a corruption of Audrey, a later form of Etheldrida.
A fair was held annually on 17 October in Ely to honour their local patron saint St Audrey who died in 679. The fair was noted initially for its fine jewellery, silver and lace, but the quality of these gradually deteriorated.

teddy bear
The soft toy is named after US President Theodore (Teddy) Roosevelt (1858–1919). He was an enthusiastic bear-hunter but was known to have spared the life of a bear cub. A cartoon showing this event later appeared in *The Washington Post*.

tradescantia
The familiar spider plant with its striped leaves is named after John Tradescant (c. 1570–1638), gardener to Charles I. He travelled widely and brought back many plants and shrubs to England.

Tuesday
The day is named in honour of Tiw, Germanic god of war.

tuxedo
This style of men's dinner jacket was first worn at Tuxedo Park Country Club in New York.

Venn diagram
This honours English mathematician, John

Venn (1834–1923), who devised the form.

volcano
The name derives from Vulcan, Roman god of fire and metal working. He also gives his name to the verb: to vulcanise.

volt
unit of electromotive force
This famously honours the name of Count Alessandro Guiseppe Antonio Anastasio Volta (1745–1827), the Italian scientist who invented the first electric battery in 1800.

watt
SI unit of power
Here James Watt (1736–1819), the Scottish engineer who developed the Newcomen steam engine, is remembered.

Wednesday
This day is named after Odin, also known as Woden or Wotan, the supreme Norse god.

wellingtons
What we know as waterproof rubber boots were originally leather boots which covered the knee and were cut away at the back. They are named after Arthur Wellesley, Duke of Wellington (1769–1852), the British soldier and Tory statesman. Known as the Iron Duke, he commanded the British in the Peninsular War (1808–14), defeated Napoleon in the Battle of Waterloo (1815) and was prime minister from 1828–1830 and again in 1834.

wistaria/wisteria
This beautiful climbing shrub honours American anatomist Caspar Wistar (1761–1818).

Yale (lock)
(trademark)
Linus Yale (1821–68), American engineer and son of a locksmith, devised the mechanism of this lock and many others. He set up the Yale Lock Manufacturing Co. in Stamford, Connecticut in 1868, the year he died.

Zeppelin
the German airship
Count Ferdinand von Zeppelin (1838–1917)

pioneered the very first airships after retiring from the army in 1891. Between 1910 and 1914 they were used to carry passengers; during World War I they were used by the Germans for reconnaissance and bombing raids over Britain.

zinnia   Let us end on a flowery note! This colourful plant was named after the very youthful German botanist and professor of medicine, Johann Gottfried Zinn (1727–59).

Unit 9:
Americanisms

Many of the differences between British English and American English will be very familiar. Sidewalk, elevator, candy, cookie, attorney, homicide are all readily translated by British readers of American literature and viewers of American films and television programmes. Not all terms, however, are understood this readily, especially when the same word has a different meaning either side of the Atlantic – shorts, purse, chips, cot, jelly, cracker, first floor, paraffin... Indeed, some differences in meaning can be deeply embarrassing for the unwary, as you will see in the list below.

There is undoubtedly a vigour in many of the American equivalents. Floor lamp, expressway, mailbox, pacifier, shoestring and stick shift are some examples of down-to-earth, straightforward words which are very appealing.

American English	British English
airplane	aeroplane
aluminum	aluminium
apartment	flat
attorney	lawyer
baby carriage	pram
baseboard	skirting board
billboard	hoarding
billfold	wallet
biscuit	scone
a blank	a form
bobby pin	hair grip
to broil	to grill
bug	insect
bulletin board	notice board
cabana	beach hut
candy	sweets
cart	trolley (supermarket)
cash on the barrel head	cash on the nail
casket	coffin
catchup/catsup	ketchup
check	bill

checkers	draughts
chips	crisps
clerk	shop assistant
clipping	cutting (from a newspaper)
closet	cupboard
collect call	reverse charge call (telephone)
comforter	eiderdown
conductor	guard (on a train)
cookie	sweet biscuit
cornstarch	cornflour
cot	camp bed
cotton candy	candyfloss
counterclockwise	anticlockwise
cracker	savoury biscuit
crib	cot
crosswalk	pedestrian crossing
cuff	turn-up (trouser)
cut-rate	cut-price
a deck	a pack (of cards)
defog	demist
diaper	nappy
divided highway	dual carriageway
downspout	drainpipe, downpipe
downtown	city centre
drapes	curtains
druggist	chemist
drugstore	chemist's shop
duplex	semi-detached house
eggplant	aubergine
eighth note	quaver
elevator	lift
engineer	engine-driver
eraser	rubber
expressway	motorway
fall	autumn
faucet	tap
fender	bumper, wing (car)
a fender-bender	a minor collision
first floor	ground floor
fish stick	fish finger
flashlight	torch

floor lamp	standard lamp
flophouse	cheap hotel/boarding house
freeway	motorway (without toll)
French fries	chips
frosting	icing
garbage	rubbish
garbage can	dustbin
gas (gasoline)	petrol
green onions	spring onions
a green thumb	green fingers
gridlock	a traffic jam
ground round	minced steak/best mince
guess	suppose
a half note	a minim
hardware store	ironmonger's
highway	main road
hobo	tramp
hog	pig
homely	plain, ugly
homicide	murder
hood	bonnet (car)
hope chest	bottom drawer
janitor	caretaker
jelly	jam
kerosene	paraffin
license plate	number plate (car)
line	queue
liquor store	off-licence
longwearing	hardwearing
lot	plot of ground
lumber	timber
mad	angry
mailbox	pillar box, post box
mean	nasty
men's room	gents
molasses	treacle
mortician	undertaker
moving man	removal man
moving van	removal van
muffler	silencer (car)
nervy	impudent

orchestra	stalls (theatre)
outlets	power points
overpass	flyover
pacifier	baby's dummy
pantyhose (pantihose)	tights
pants	trousers
paraffin	paraffin wax
parking lot	car park
pavement	tarmac, asphalt surface
pie	tart
pin	brooch
pitcher	jug
podiatrist	chiropodist
porch	verandah
pot holder	oven glove
purse	handbag
quarter note	crotchet
railroad	railway
a raise	a rise (salary)
real estate	property
realtor	estate agent
rest room	lavatory
résumé	curriculum vitae (CV)
roomer	lodger
rooster	cock
rotary	roundabout (traffic)
round-trip ticket	return ticket
rowboat	rowing boat
row house	terraced house
rubber	condom
rummage sale	jumble sale
rutabaga	swede
sanitarium	sanatorium
second floor	first floor
sedan	saloon (car)
shoestring	shoelace
shorts	men's underpants
sidewalk	pavement
sink	washbasin, hand basin
slingshot	catapult
sneakers	plimsolls/trainers

snow pea	mangetout
soda	fizzy drink
spool	cotton reel
station wagon	estate car
stick shift	gearstick
stop light	traffic lights
store	shop
streetcar	tram
stroller	pushchair
substitute teacher	supply teacher
subway	underground
suspenders	braces
talk show	chat show
teeter-totter	seesaw
tempest in a teapot	storm in a teacup
thumbtack	drawing pin
tick-tack-toe/tic-tac-toe	noughts and crosses
traffic circle	roundabout
trailer	caravan
trailer park	caravan/mobile home site
trash	rubbish
trash can	dustbin
truck	lorry
trucker	lorry driver
truck farm	market garden
truck stop	transport café
trunk	boot (car)
tub	bath
two weeks	fortnight
underpants	knickers
undershirt	vest
vacation	holiday
vacationer	holidaymaker
valence	pelmet
vest	waistcoat
visor	peak (of cap)
washroom	lavatory, public toilet
to wash up	to wash hands and face
window shade	window blind
windshield	windscreen
yard	back garden

zip code	postcode
zipper	zip
zucchini	courgette

TEST YOUR WORD POWER

Translate into British English these Americanisms.

1. podiatrist   _____
2. résumé   _____
3. realtor   _____
4. roomer   _____
5. mean   _____
6. homely   _____
7. nervy   _____
8. mad   _____
9. biscuit   _____
10. chips   _____
11. ground round   _____
12. rutabaga   _____
13. pants   _____
14. shorts   _____
15. underpants   _____
16. undershirt   _____
17. checkers   _____
18. slingshot   _____
19. teeter-totter   _____
20. tick-tack-toe   _____

Translate into American English these British expressions.

21. pushchair   _____

22. pram   _____

23. cot   _____

24. nappy   _____

25. saloon car   _____

26. gearstick   _____

27. silencer   _____

28. petrol   _____

29. tights   _____

30. braces   _____

31. waistcoat   _____

32. trouser turn-up   _____

33. market garden   _____

34. car park   _____

35. caravan site   _____

36. transport café   _____

37. pedestrian crossing   _____

38. dual carriageway   _____

39. traffic roundabout   _____

40. pavement   _____

Complete the gaps in the table below.

	British English	**American English**
41.	drawing pin	_____
42.	wallet	_____
43.	spring onions	_____
44.	tap	_____

45. cupboard _____

46. _____ duplex

47. _____ baseboard

48. _____ to broil

49. _____ cabana

50. _____ comforter

Score:_____/50

Unit 10:
Foreign Words and Phrases in English

It is surprising how many foreign words and phrases are used in everyday modern English. Some have survived in the language through long tradition; others have been admitted because there is no adequate concise English equivalent.

Nearly 500 words and phrases are listed alphabetically here. You can test your understanding at the end of the unit.

ab initio (Latin)	from the start
ab ovo (Latin)	(lit. 'from the egg') from the very beginning
Achtung! (German)	Look out! Take care!
addendum (sing.) (Latin) **addenda** (plural)	(lit. 'that which is to be added') material added after the main text has been completed
à deux (French)	(lit. 'for two') romantic, intimate
ad hoc (Latin)	(lit. 'for this') for one particular purpose
ad infinitum (Latin)	(lit. 'without limit') endlessly
ad nauseam (Latin)	(lit. 'to the point of causing (sea) sickness') excessively
affaire de coeur (French)	romantic relationship
aficionado (Spanish)	someone who takes an enthusiastic and well-informed interest in a subject/sport/ hobby
a fortiori (Latin)	all the more, with stronger reason
agent provocateur (French)	(lit. 'provocative agent') someone who leads others into illegal actions for which they will be punished
aggiornamento (Italian)	(lit. 'bringing up to today') modernisation, reform

aide-de-camp (French)
(ADC)
(lit. 'assistant in the field')
personal assistant to an officer

aide-mémoire (French)
(lit. 'help memory')
something that helps you to remember

à la (French)
in the style of

à la carte (French)
(lit. 'on the menu')
with each dish chosen separately and priced individually

à la mode (French)
fashionable

al dente (Italian)
(lit. 'to the tooth')
boiled but still firm when bitten

alfresco (Italian)
(lit. 'in the fresh')
in the fresh air; in the open

alma mater (Latin)
(lit. 'nourishing mother')
the school, college or university someone attended

alter ego (Latin)
(lit. 'another I')
second self; soul-mate; inseparable friend; bosom pal

alumnus (masc.)
alumna (fem.) (Latin)
alumni/
alumnae (plural)
(lit. 'foster child')
past student or graduate

ambiance
surroundings, atmosphere of a place
(sometimes anglicised – ambience)

amende honorable
  (French)
(lit. 'honourable reparation')
public apology

amour (French)
(lit. 'love')
love affair (esp. one kept secret)

amour propre (French)
(lit. 'own love')
self-respect, self-esteem

angst (German, Danish)
(lit. 'fear')
acute but unattributable feeling of apprehension and foreboding; feeling of alarm

anno Domini (Latin)
(A.D.)
in the year of our Lord
(i.e. dating from the birth of Christ)

annus horribilis (Latin) (lit. 'horrible year')

annus mirabilis (Latin) (lit. 'marvellous year')

anschauung (German)   (lit. 'way of looking at things') point of view, attitude

anschluss (German)   (lit. 'joining together') union (of countries)

ante meridiem (Latin) (lit. 'before noon') (a.m.)

ante partum (Latin)   (lit. 'before birth')

aperçu (French)   (lit. 'what has been perceived') an insight; a penetrating comment

apologia pro vita sua (Latin)   (lit. 'a defence of his/her life') a written justification of one's beliefs and actions

a posteriori (Latin)   (lit. 'from what comes after') describes reasoning based on experience or observation

appellation contrôlée (French)   (lit. 'certified name') (of wine)

a priori (Latin)   (lit. 'from what comes first') describes reasoning based on cause and effect

à propos (French)   (lit. 'to the purpose') on the subject, with reference

arriviste (French)   (lit. 'someone arriving') a person who is unscrupulously ambitious

attaché (French)   (lit. 'someone attached') a specialist attached to a diplomatic mission

au contraire (French) (lit. 'to the contrary')

au courant (French)   (lit. 'in the current') bring up to date with latest developments; knowing what is going on

au fait (French)   (lit. 'to the point;) knowledgeable; familiar with something

au fond (French)   (lit. 'at the bottom') fundamentally; essentially

auf Wiedersehen
  (German)

(lit. 'until we see each other again')
goodbye

au naturel (French)

(lit. 'in a natural condition')
naked; uncooked

au pair (French)

(lit. 'on an equal footing')
young foreigner helping with children and
household tasks (with the purpose of
learning the language) in exchange for
board, lodging and pocket money

au revoir (French)

(lit. 'until we see each other again')
goodbye

avant-garde (French)

(lit. 'front guard;)
sympathising with modern, advanced ideas

bain-marie (French)

(lit. 'Mary's bath')
a double saucepan

baksheesh
  (from Persian)

(lit. 'something given')
a tip, a present, a bribe (in some Eastern
countries)

beau geste (French)

(lit. 'beautiful gesture')
a generous or unselfish act

beau idéal (French)

(lit. 'ideal beauty')
the perfect type; a perfect model; a
beautiful idea!

beau monde (French)

(lit. 'beautiful world')
fashionable people

belle époque (French)

(lit. 'the beautiful epoch')
time of gracious living (for the wealthy)
before World War I

belles lettres (French)

(lit. 'beautiful letters')
works of literature valued more for their
style than for their content

bête noire (French)

(lit. 'black beast')
someone or something that one particularly
dislikes or dreads

bildungsroman
  (German)

(lit. 'educational novel')
a novel concerning the formative years of
its central character

billet doux (French)   (lit. 'a sweet letter')
a love letter

blasé (French)   (lit. 'cloyed')
bored by over-familiarity

blitzkreig (German)   (lit. 'lightning war')
a swift military attack designed to defeat
the enemy quickly

bona fides (Latin)   (lit. 'good faith')
a *bona fide* offer is a genuine one

bonhomie (French)   (from 'bon homme' = good man)
good-natured friendliness

bon mot (French)   (lit. 'good word')
a witty remark

bon vivant (French)   (lit. 'good-living person')
someone who enjoys the fine things of life

bon voyage (French)   (lit. 'good journey')

bouclé (French)   (lit. 'curly')
a curled, knobbly yarn

bouffant (French)   (lit. 'puffed out')
back-combed hair
puffed out (sleeves, skirt)

bouillon (French)   (from 'bouillir' to boil)
plain broth or stock

bourgeois (French)   (lit. 'someone who lives in a town')
middle-class, conventional

brouhaha (French)   commotion; uproar

canaille (French)   (lit. 'pack of dogs')
mob; rabble; the masses

canard (French)   (lit. 'duck')
an untrue report; false rumour

Carpe diem. (Latin)   (lit. 'Seize the day.')
Enjoy the pleasures of the present moment
while they last and don't worry about the
future.

carte blanche (French)   (lit. 'blank sheet of paper')
complete freedom to do what one wants

casus belli (Latin) — (lit. 'occasion of war')
justification for making war; the circumstances or situation that leads to war

cause célèbre (French) — (lit. 'trial which arouses public interest')
a matter which attracts attention and causes controversy

Caveat emptor. (Latin) — (lit. 'Let the buyer beware.')

C'est la vie! (French) — (lit. 'That's life!')

chacun à son goût — (lit. 'each to his own tastes')

chambré (French) — (lit. 'having been put in a room')
brought to room temperature

chargé d'affaires (French) — (lit. 'in charge of business')
an ambassador's deputy or substitute

chef d'oeuvre (French) — (lit. 'chief work')
a writer's or artist's masterpiece

Cherchez la femme. (French) — (lit. 'Look for the woman.')

chez (French) — (lit. 'at the home of')

chiaroscuro (Italian) — (lit. 'clear and obscure')
artistic distribution of light and dark masses

chutzpah (Yiddish) — impudence; shameless audacity

ciao (Italian) — (lit. 'I am your slave.')
informal greeting on meeting and parting

cinéma-verité (French) — (lit. 'truth cinema')
realism in films

circa (Latin) (c.) — (lit. 'around')
approximately (of dates)

cognoscente (sing.)
cognoscenti (plural) (Italian) — (lit. 'one who knows')
connoisseur, person with informed appreciation in a field of the arts

comme il faut (French) — (lit. 'as it is necessary')
correct (behaviour)

compos mentis (Latin) — (lit. 'in control of the mind')
of sound mind

con amore (Italian) — (lit. 'with love')
lovingly

contretemps (French) (lit. 'against time')
an awkward situation; an embarrassing disagreement

cordon bleu (French) (lit. 'blue ribbon')
describes cooking of the highest standard

cordon sanitaire
  (French) (lit. 'sanitary line')
line isolating an infected area; line of buffer states shielding a country

corrigendum (sing.)⎫
corrigenda (plural)⎭ Latin (lit. 'item(s) to be corrected')

coup d'état (French) (lit. 'blow of state')
the unexpected overthrow of a government

coup de foudre
  (French) (lit. 'flash of lightning')
a sudden and astonishing happening

coup de grâce (French) (lit. 'blow of mercy')
a final or decisive stroke

coup d'oeil (French) (lit. 'blow of the eye')
a quick look; a glance

crème de la crème
  (French) (lit. 'cream of the cream')
the very best

cri de coeur (French) (lit. 'cry from the heart')
a heartfelt appeal

crime passionnel
  (French) (lit. 'crime relating to the passions')
crime of passion; murder as a result of sexual jealousy

Cui bono? (Latin) (lit. 'To whom for a benefit?')
Who stands to gain?

cum laude (Latin) (lit. 'with praise')
An American degree awarded 'cum laude' is the equivalent of third class.
See also **summa cum laude** and **magna cum laude**.

curriculum vitae
  (C.V.) (Latin) (lit. 'course of one's life')
a written account of one's qualifications and experience in support of a job application

débâcle (French) (lit. 'an unbolting')
a sudden disastrous defeat or collapse

déclassé (m.) ⎫ (French) **déclasseé** (f.) ⎭	(lit. 'out of one's class') someone who has come down in the world	

décolleté (French) low-cut (of the neckline of a dress or blouse)

de facto (Latin) (lit. 'from the fact')
actually, though not necessarily legally

de iure/de jure (Latin) sanctioned by law; legally

déjà vu (French) (lit. 'already seen')
the feeling that one has experienced something before the present in which it is happening

delirium tremens (D.T.s) (Latin) (lit. 'trembling delirium')
'the shakes' – the result of alcoholic over-indulgence over a long period

de luxe (French) (lit. 'of luxury')
superior in quality

demi-monde (French) (lit. 'half-world')
a stratum of society considered to be not wholly respectable
(half-in and half-out!)

démodé (French) (lit. 'out of fashion')

demi-pension (French) half-board (of accommodation)

dénouement (French) (lit. 'untying of the knot')
the resolution of the plot of a play or story; the outcome

de novo (Latin) (lit. 'for new')
anew (as in 'a fresh start')

Deo gratias (Latin) (D.G.) (lit. 'thanks be to God')

Deo volente (Latin) (D.V.) (lit. 'God willing')

de profundis (Latin) (lit. 'from the depths')

déraciné (French) (lit. 'uprooted')
removed from one's geographical and social background

de rigueur (French) (lit. 'of strictness')
what is required by social convention

dernier cri (French)   (lit. 'last cry')
the latest fashion

derrière (French)   (lit. 'behind')
the behind; the buttocks

déshabillé (French)   (lit. 'undressed')
only partially dressed; casually dressed

de trop (French)   (lit. 'of too much')
unwanted; in the way

deus ex machina (Latin)   (lit. 'a god out of the machine')
an unlikely solution to a problem; an unexpected intervention when disaster seemed inevitable

distingué (French)   (lit. 'distinguished')
of a noble or striking appearance

distrait (French)   absent-minded; slightly worried and disorganised

dolce far niente
(Italian)   (lit. 'sweet doing nothing')
the pleasure of doing nothing; in a soft smooth way (musical)

donnée (French)   (lit. 'that which is given')
a basic fact or assumption

doppelgänger (German)   (lit. 'a double-goer')
a double; someone who looks exactly like someone else (and may be mistaken for him or her)

double entendre
(French)   (lit. 'to hear twice')
a remark with two possible meanings, one of which is usually sexually suggestive

doyen (m.) } (French)   (lit. 'dean')
doyenne (f.)   the most distinguished member of a profession, branch of the arts, etc.

dramatis personae
(Latin)   (lit. 'persons of the drama')
cast of characters

droit de seigneur
(French)   (lit. 'the right of the lord')
the alleged right of a feudal lord to sleep with a serf's bride on the night before her wedding

dummkopf (German)   (lit. 'stupid head')
idiot; blockhead

echt (German)   (lit. 'real, genuine')

éclat (French)   (lit. 'explosion')
great acclaim; brilliant success

élan French)   (lit. 'rush, dash')
flair; impressive, energetic style

embarras de richesse   (lit. 'embarrassment of wealth')
(French)   having too much money; having more than
you need of anything nice

embonpoint (French)   (lit. 'in good condition')
stoutness; plumpness

emeritus (Latin)   (lit. 'having served one's term')
retired from full-time work but retaining
one's title on an honorary basis

éminence grise (French)   (lit. 'grey eminence')
someone who exerts great power behind
the scenes without official status

en bloc (French)   (lit. 'in a block')
all together

en famille (French)   (lit. 'in the family')
with one's family; informally

enfant terrible (French)   (lit. 'terrible child')
adult with a reputation for unconventional
and embarrassing behaviour on public
occasions

en fête (French)   (lit. 'in festival')
dressed for festivity; engaged in a festivity

en masse (French)   (lit. 'in a mass')
all together as a unit

ennui (French)   a feeling of listlessness or boredom arising
from inactivity and lack of involvement

en passant (French)   (lit. 'in passing')
by the way; incidentally

en route (French)   (lit. 'on the way')

entente cordiale (French)	(lit. 'a cordial understanding') a friendly understanding between two political powers
entre nous (French)	(lit. 'between us') confidentially
épater les bourgeois (French)	to shock the middle-class (e.g. by an unconventional art exhibition or theatrical production)
ergo (Latin)	therefore
erratum (sing.) ⎱ (Latin) **errata** (plural) ⎰	an error/errors
ersatz (German)	(lit. 'substitute') cheap substitute; inferior substitute
esprit de corps (French)	(lit. 'spirit of a group') team spirit
(et al.) **et alia** (Latin)	(lit. 'and others')
(etc.) **et cetera** (Latin)	(lit. 'and the rest')
ex cathedra (Latin)	(lit. 'from the chair') with authority
exeat (Latin)	(lit. 'let him or her go forth') permission to be absent (e.g. for a weekend from a boarding school)
exempli gratia (Latin) (e.g.)	for instance
ex gratia (Latin)	(lit. 'from favour') given without legal obligation to be given (e.g. an ex-gratia payment)
ex libris (Latin)	(lit. 'from the books (of)') from the library (of)
ex more (Latin)	by custom; according to custom
ex officio (Latin)	by virtue of one's official position
ex parte (Latin)	from one side only (in legal proceedings)
extempore (Latin)	(lit. 'out of time') without preparation

fait accompli (French)   (lit. 'an accomplished fact')
something that has been done that cannot
be undone or changed in any way

farouche (French)   (lit. 'from out of doors')
wild; shy; untamed; sullen

fatwa (Arabic)   a religious decree proclaimed by a Muslim
leader

faux pas (French)   (lit. 'false step')
social blunder

felo de se (Latin)   (lit. 'one who commits a crime against
himself or herself')
suicide (legal)

femme fatale (French)   (lit. 'fatal woman')
a woman whose seductive charms lead men
to be compromised and destroyed

festina lente (French)   (lit. 'make haste slowly')

fête champêtre (French)   (lit. 'rustic festival')
grand open-air party

fin de siècle (French)   (lit. 'end of the century')
used of the end of the C19th and its
perceived artistic decadence

flambé (French)   (lit. 'flamed')
used of food served in flaming spirits,
usually brandy

flâneur (French)   an idler; a wastrel

folie de grandeur
  (French)   delusions of grandeur

fons et origo (Latin)   (lit. 'source and origin')

fracas (French)   a brawl; a noisy quarrel

frisson (French)   (lit. 'a shiver')
a pleasurable shiver of fear or excitement

führer (German)   (lit. 'leader', esp. Hitler)
used to desribe anyone who behaves
autocratically towards subordinates

furore (Latin)   a public outburst

gamine (French)   a slim and boyish girl or young woman

gauleiter (German)   a petty tyrant

gemütlich (German)   (lit. 'comfortable')
cosy; comfortable; nice

genre (French)   (lit. 'kind' or 'type')
a particular kind of music, literature or art

gesundheit (German)   (lit. 'health')
traditionally uttered when someone sneezes
like 'bless you'

glasnost (Russian)   (lit. 'publicity')
policy of public frankness and
accountability

gratis (Latin)   (lit. 'out of kindness')
free

gravitas (Latin)   (lit. 'weight')
authority; seriousness or solemnity of
demeanour and conduct

gulag (Russian)   any system used for silencing dissidents; a
corrective camp

guru (Hindi)   (from Sanskrit: 'weighty')
a Hindu or Sikh spiritual leader; a leader of
a religious cult; a leading authority

habitué (French)   a frequent visitor to a place

haute couture (French)   (lit. 'high dressmaking')
high fashion

haut monde (French)   (lit. 'high world')
high society

hic iacet/hic jacet (Latin) here lies

hoi polloi (Greek)   (lit. 'the many')
the masses; the common people

homo sapiens (Latin)   (lit. 'wise man')
the scientific name for modern man

hors concours (French) (lit. 'out of the competition')
unequalled; peerless; not competing for an
award

hors de combat
   (French)   (lit. 'out of the fight')
injured; disabled; not able to take part

hors d'oeuvre (sing.)   (lit. 'outside the work')

hors d'oeuvres (plural) an appetiser, served before the main course
  (French)

hwyl (Welsh)   emotional fervour

(ibid) **ibidem** (Latin)   (lit. 'in the same place')
                                     in the same book, article, passage, etc.

idée fixe (French)   (lit. 'a fixed idea')
                                     an obsession

(id) **idem** (Latin)   (lit. 'the same')
                                     ditto

(i.e.) **id est** (Latin)   (lit. 'it is')
                                     that is (used before a clarification of a
                                     statement)

in absentia (Latin)   (lit. 'in absence')
                                     in a person's absence

inamorato (m.) ⎱(Italian) a person with whom one is in love
inamorata (f.) ⎰

in articulo mortis   (lit. 'in the grasp of death')
  (Latin)   at the point of death

in camera (Latin)   (lit. 'in a chamber')
                                     in private (legal)

incommunicado   deprived of communication with other
  (Spanish)   people

in extremis (Latin)   (lit. 'in the last')
                                     at the point of death; in dire straits

in flagrante delicto   (lit. 'with the crime blazing')
  (Latin)   caught in the act; caught red-handed

(infra dig) **infra**   (lit. 'below dignity')
dignitatem (Latin)   beneath one's dignity

ingénue (French)   inexperienced young girl

in loco parentis (Latin) (lit. 'in the place of a parent')

in memoriam (Latin)   (lit. 'in memory')

in perpetuum (Latin)   forever

in propria persona   (lit. 'in one's own person')
  (Latin)   personally, in person

in situ (Latin)   in position; in the appropriate place

inter alia (Latin)   (lit. 'among other things')

interregnum (Latin) a period between rulers

In vino veritas. (Latin) (lit. 'In wine there is truth.')
Alcohol will loosen the tongue.

in vitro (Latin) (lit. 'in glass')
in a test-tube

ipso facto (Latin) by that very fact

je ne sais quoi (French) (lit. 'I don't know what')
an indefinable something

jeu d'esprit (French) (lit. 'play of spirit')
a light-hearted display of wit or brilliance,
especially in literature

jeunesse dorée
(French) (lit. 'gilded youth')
privileged, fashionable and wealthy young
people

jihad (Arabic) (lit. 'conflict')
a holy war undertaken by Muslims against
infidels

joie de vivre (French) (lit. 'joy of living')
enjoyment of life

kamikaze (Japanese) (lit. 'divine wind')
describing an action or a person willing to
die in inflicting maximum destruction on
the enemy; a suicide bomber

kaput (German) (lit. 'done for')
ruined; broken; completely destroyed

karaoke (Japanese) (lit. 'empty orchestra')
an entertainment where members of the
public take it in turns to sing well-known
songs over a pre-recorded backing

karma (Sanskrit) (lit. 'action, effort')
force produced by the way one lives one's
life which will affect subsequent
reincarnations

kitsch (German) tawdry; vulgar; tasteless

lacrimae rerum (Latin) (lit. 'the tears of things')
sorrow at the heart of life

la dolce vita (Italian)   (lit. 'the sweet life')
luxurious and licentious lifestyle

laissez-faire (French)   (lit. 'let do')
a policy of non-interference

lapsus linguae (Latin)   (lit. 'a slip of the tongue')

lebensraum (German)   (lit. 'living space')

leitmotif (German)   (lit. 'leading motive')
a recurrent image or theme

lèse majesté (French)   (lit. 'injured majesty')
treason; any attack on authority

lingua franca (Latin)   (lit. 'Frankish tongue')
simplified language used for communication
with people speaking different languages;
common basis for understanding not
requiring language (ballet, etc.)

literati (Latin)   well-educated people who are interested in
literature

locum tenens (Latin)
(locum)   (lit. 'holding the place')
a person who stands in temporarily for
another member of the same profession
(doctor, dentist, chemist, etc.)

magna cum laude
(Latin)   (lit. 'with great praise')
second class honours in an American degree

magnum opus (Latin)   (lit. 'big work')
a person's artistic masterpiece

mal de mer (French)   (lit. 'sickness of the sea')

mañana (Spanish)   (lit. 'tomorrow')
the inclination to put anything demanding
off to a later date; living for the moment

manqué (French)   (lit. 'having missed')
unfulfilled; with potential unrealised

mariage blanc
(French)   (lit. 'white marriage')
an unconsummated marriage

materfamilias (Latin)   (lit. 'mother of a family')
matriarch

mea culpa (Latin)   (lit. 'through my fault')
I am to blame.

mêlée French)	confused mass of people
memento mori (Latin)	(lit. 'remember that you must die') an object such as a skull which reminds one that death is inevitable
ménage à trois (French)	(lit. 'household of three') a married couple and the lover of the husband or wife living together
mens sana in corpore sano (Latin)	(lit. 'a healthy mind in a healthy body')
métier (French)	one's profession or trade
milieu (French)	setting, location
mirabile dictu (Latin)	(lit. 'wonderful to say')
modus operandi (Latin)	(lit. 'way of working')
modus vivendi (Latin)	(lit. 'way of living') a practical compromise between two conflicting protagonists; a working arrangement
mot juste (French)	(lit. 'the exact word')
multum in parvo (Latin)	(lit. 'much in little') a lot in a small space
mutatis mutandis (Latin)	(lit. 'things having been changed which needed to be changed') having made the necessary changes
nada (Spanish)	nothing
naïveté (French)	ingenuous behaviour
née French)	(lit. 'born') precedes the maiden name of a married woman
(nem. con.) **nemine contradicente** (Latin)	**(lit. 'with no one contradicting')**
ne plus ultra (Latin)	(lit. 'not more beyond') perfection
nihil obstat (Latin)	(lit. 'nothing stands in the way')
nil desperandum (Latin)	(lit. 'nothing is to be despaired of')
nisi (Latin)	(lit. 'unless')

Noli me tangere. (Latin) (lit. 'Do not touch me.')

nom de plume (French) (lit. 'a name of the pen')
pen name, pseudonym

non compos mentis (lit. 'not in control of one's mind')
(Latin)

non sequitur (Latin) (lit. 'it does not follow')
an illogical step in an argument

nostalgie de la boue (lit. 'a yearning for mud')
(French) a craving for a debased physical life
(often for sexual degradation)

nota bene (Latin) (lit. 'note well')
(N.B.) note carefully

nouveau riche (French) (lit. 'new rich')
someone who has recently become wealthy
but lacks social graces

nouvelle cuisine (lit. 'new cooking')
(French) a style of cooking based on the attractive
visual presentation of lightly cooked
ingredients

objet d'art (French) (lit. 'an object of art')
small object considered to be of artistic
merit

objet trouvé (French) (lit. 'a found object')
a natural object (stone, branch, etc.) which
is considered to be of artistic merit and
displayed as such

opere citato (Latin) (lit. 'in the work cited')
(op. cit.)

opus (Latin) (lit. 'the work')
an artistic composition or musical work

outré (French) (lit. 'beyond')
beyond what is proper and conventionally
acceptable

pace (Latin) (lit. 'with peace')
with due deference to

panem et circenses (Latin)
(lit. 'bread and circuses')
amusements to distract the masses from unpleasant realities

paparazzo (sing.)
paparazzi (plural) (Italian)
freelance photographer(s) who specialise(s) in sensational photographs of the rich and famous

par excellence (French)
(lit. 'by way of excellence')
beyond comparison

parvenu (French)
an upstart; a person of low social position who suddenly acquires wealth or celebrity

passé (French)
(lit. 'past')
out-of-date; old-fashioned

passim (Latin)
(lit. 'scattered here and there')
occurring throughout a work

paterfamilias (Latin)
(lit. 'father of a family')
head of an extended family; patriarch

patois (French)
dialect; jargon of a particular group

pax (Latin)
(lit. 'peace')

per annum (Latin)
(lit. 'by the year')
annually

per capita (Latin)
(lit. 'by the head')
for each person

per diem (Latin)
(lit. 'by the day')
daily

perestroika (Russian)
(lit. 'reconstruction')
restructuring the economy of a country

per procurationem (per pro. or p.p.) (Latin)
(lit. 'by delegation')
used when signing documents on behalf of someone else

per se (Latin)
(lit. 'by itself')
intrinsically

persona non grata (Latin)
(lit. 'unacceptable person')

pièce de résistance (French)
the main dish of a meal; the principal or most outstanding achievement of somebody

pied à terre (French)	(lit. 'foot on the ground') a flat or small dwelling for occasional use
pinxit (Latin)	(lit. 'he/she painted (it)')
Plus ça change, plus c'est la même chose. (French)	(lit. 'The more things change, the more things stay the same.')
post meridiem (p.m.) (Latin)	(lit. 'after noon')
post partum (Latin)	(lit. 'after the birth')
post scriptum (Latin) (P.S.)	(lit. 'after the writing') a postscript
pour encourager les autres (French)	(lit. 'to encourage the others')
premier cru (French)	(lit. 'first growth')
prêt-à-porter (French)	(lit. 'ready-to-wear')
prima facie (Latin)	(lit. 'at first sight')
primus inter pares (Latin)	(lit. 'first among equals')
prix fixe (French)	(lit. 'fixed price') describes a meal in a restaurant offered at an all-inclusive price
pro bono publico (Latin)	(lit. 'for the public good')
pro patria (Latin)	(lit. 'for one's country')
pro rata (Latin)	proportionately
pro tempore (Latin) (pro tem)	for the time being
putsch (Swiss German)	(lit. 'a thrust') a secretly planned sudden attempt to depose a government; a political revolt
qua (Latin)	in the capacity of
Que serà serà. (Spanish)	(lit. 'Whatever will be will be.')
quid pro quo (Latin)	(lit. 'something for something')
Quis custodiet ipsos custodies? (Latin)	(lit. 'Who will guard the guards?')

Quod erat demonstrandum. (Q.E.D.) (Latin) We have proved the proposition that we have set out to prove.

(q.v.) quod vide (Latin) (lit. 'which see')
see

quondam (Latin) former

Quo vadis? (Latin) (lit. 'Where are you going?)

raconteur (French) person skilled in telling stories

raison d'être (French) reason for existence

rapprochement (French) (lit. 'bringing together again')

rara avis (Latin) (lit. 'a rare bird')
something or someone very unusual

realpolitik (German) (lit. 'politics of realism')

réchauffé (French) (lit. 'heated up again')

recherché (French) (lit. 'searched for')
choice; rare; known only to connoisseurs

réclame (French) public acclaim; publicity

recto (Latin) right-hand page of a book

Répondez, s'il vous plaît. (French) (R.S.V.P.) (lit. 'Please reply.')

Requiescat in pace. (sing.) (Latin)
Requiescant. (plural) (R.I.P.) (Latin) (lit. 'May he/she/they rest in peace.')

retroussé (French) turned-up (nose)

Revenons à nos moutons (French) (lit. 'Let us return to our sheep')
Let's get back to the main point.

risqué (French) (lit. 'risky')
bordering on impropriety

roman à clef (French) (lit. 'a novel with a key')
a novel based on thinly-disguised real people whom the initiated will recognise.

routier (French) a long-distance lorry driver

rus in urbe (Latin) (lit. 'the country in the town')

sanctum sanctorum (Latin)   (lit. 'holy of holies')

sang-froid (French)   (lit. 'cold blood')
composure; self-possession

sans cérémonie (French)   (lit. 'without ceremony')

sauté (French)   (lit. 'tossed')
to fry food quickly

savoir faire (French)   (lit. 'to know how to do')
the ability to do the right thing in a situation

schadenfreude (German)   (lit. 'harm and joy')
taking pleasure in the misery of others

schmalz (German)   excessive sentimentality

semper fidelis (Latin)   (lit. 'faithful for ever')

sequens (sing.) ⎫
sequentes (plural) ⎬(Latin)   the following
(seq. or seqq.) ⎭

seriatim (Latin)   in series

sic (Latin)   thus
used in parenthesis to indicate a mistake made by an author in a passage being quoted by another writer

sine die (Latin)   (lit. 'without a day')
until an unspecified date

sine qua non (Latin)   (lit. 'without which not')
an indispensable condition; something that cannot be done without

soi-disant (French)   (lit. 'oneself-calling')
so-called

soigné (m) ⎫(French)   (lit. 'looked after')
soignée (f) ⎭   beautifully groomed

soirée (French)   an evening entertainment

sotto voce (Italian)   (lit. 'under the voice')
speaking quietly in an undertone

soubriquet (French)   a nickname

soupçon (French) — (lit. 'suspicion')
a faint trace; a minute amount

status quo (Latin) — as things stand; the present state of affairs

stet (Latin) — (lit. 'let it stand')
an editor's or proofreader's mark cancelling a deletion or alteration

sub iudice ⎫
sub judice ⎬(Latin) — (lit. 'under the judge')
indicates that an action is still being considered in a court of law and so should pass without comment

subpoena (Latin) — (lit. 'under penalty')
a legal summons to appear in court

sub rosa (Latin) — (lit. 'under the rose')
in strict confidence

succès de scandale (French) — (lit. 'success of scandal')
a book, painting, film which is successful as a result of its scandalous subject matter rather than through its own merit

sui generis (Latin) — (lit. 'of its own kind')
in a class of its own; unique

summa cum laude (Latin) — first class honours in an American degree

table d'hôte (French) — (lit. 'at the host's table')
a set of dishes in a restaurant at a set price

tabula rasa (Latin) — (lit. 'a scraped writing tablet')
a clean slate (on which life has yet to leave its marks)

Tempus fugit. (Latin) — (lit. 'Time flies.')

terra firma (Latin) — (lit. 'firm earth')
dry land

tête-à-tête (French) — (lit. 'head to head')
a private conversation

touché (French) — (lit. 'touched')
used as an acknowledgement of a witty reply or remark that has made its mark

tour de force (French) — a remarkable feat or achievement

tout court (French)   (lit. 'quite short')
just that and nothing else

toute de suite (French) immediately

tout le monde (French) everybody

trompe l'oeil (French)   (lit. 'deceives the eye')
a painting that gives a convincing illusion
of reality
(e.g. a window and the scene through it
painted on the wall of a room)

ultra vires (Latin)   (lit. 'beyond strength')
beyond the legal authority of

urbi et orbi (Latin)   (lit. 'to the city and to the world')

vade mecum (Latin)   (lit. 'go with me')
a handbook or other aid carried by a
person for immediate easy reference

Veni, vidi, vici. (Latin) (lit. 'I came, I saw, I conquered.')

verbatim (Latin)   (lit. 'word for word')

verboten (German)   (lit. 'forbidden')

verso (Latin)   the left-hand page of a book

(v.) **versus** (Latin)   against

via (Latin)   by way of

vice versa (Latin)   (lit. 'the change being turned')
conversely

(viz) **videlicet** (Latin)   (lit. 'it is permitted to see')
namely

vin du pays (French)   (lit. 'wine of the country')
locally produced wine

vis-à-vis (French)   (lit. 'face to face')
in relation to

Vivat. (Latin)   (lit. 'May he/she live.')
Long live.

viva voce (Latin)   (lit. 'with the living voice')
orally

volte-face (French)   (lit. 'turn face')
a reversal; a U-turn

wagonlit (French)   a sleeping car on a European railway

wanderlust (German)   (lit. 'wander-desire')
an irresistible urge to travel

weltanschauung   (lit. 'world perception')
   (German)   a particular philosophy or view of life

weltschmerz (German)   (lit. 'world pain')
a feeling of melancholy and world-
weariness

wunderkind (German)   (lit. 'wonder child')
a child prodigy

Zeitgeist (German)   (lit. 'time spirit')
the characteristic outlook at a particular
time in history

TEST YOUR WORD POWER

Complete this table of abbreviations.

1. A.D.   _____   in the year of our Lord

2. a.m.   _____   before noon

3. c.   circa   _____

4. C.V.   _____   resumé of qualifications

5. D.G.   Deo gratias   _____

6. D.V.   Deo volente   _____

7. e.g.   exempli gratia   _____

8. et al.   et alia   _____

9. etc.   _____   and so on

10. _____   ibidem   as previously cited

11. i.e.   id est   _____

12. _____   nemine contradicente   unanimously

13. N.B.   nota bene   _____

14. _____   opera citato   in the work already quoted

15. p.a.   _____   annually

16. p.m.   _____   after noon

17. _____ per procurationem   signed on behalf of

18. P.S. _____   added to the letter

19. pro tem.   pro tempore   _____

20. Q.E.D. _____   what has to be proved has been proved

21. q.v.   quod vide   _____

22. R.I.P.   Requiescat in pace.   _____

23. R.S.V.P. Répondez, s'il vous plait. _____

24. _____ sequens   the following

25. _____ videlicet   namely

Supply the missing words in these foreign phrases.

26. Caveat _____ .   (Let the buyer beware.)

27. mirabile_____   (wonderful to relate)

28. _____ de plume   (a pen name)

29. savoir   _____   (social expertise; knowing what to say at the right time)

30. _____ de force   (a remarkable achievement)

What are these?

31. a billet doux   _____

32. an aperçu   _____

33. a double entendre   _____

34. a tête-à-tête   _____

35. joie de vivre   _____

36. sang-froid   _____

37. an aide-memoire   _____

38. a bête noire   _____

39. schadenfreude   _____

40.   an affaire de coeur _____

Match up these foreign words and phrases with the correct definition by drawing a connecting line between them.

41.	folie de grandeur	a double saucepan
42.	inamorata	plumpness
43.	lapsus linguae	uneasy anxious forebording
44.	doppelgänger	a brawl
45.	angst	a spiritual leader
46.	guru	a witticism
47.	embonpoint	a sweetheart
48.	bain-marie	a slip of the tongue
49.	bon mot	delusions of greatness
50.	fracas	a double

Score:_____/50

Unit 11:
Proverbs

Proverbs are brief, pithy sayings:

▶ A fool and his money are soon parted.

▶ A miss is as good as a mile.

▶ Don't count your chickens before they're hatched.

The origins of most of our proverbs are lost in the mists of time, although a few are Biblical in origin (The spirit is willing but the flesh is weak), a few are literary (Cowards die many times before their death) and a few are based on Greek and Latin originals (Better late than never).

Proverbs are fascinating. They are part of our linguistic currency, widely known and widely used. Their popular wisdom makes them as relevant to the present day as they have been in the centuries they span. Rhyme, rhythm, alliteration and succinctness help to make them easy to remember:

▶ Waste not, want not.

▶ Look before you leap.

▶ An apple a day keeps the doctor away.

▶ There's many a slip 'twixt the cup and the lip.

Here are some proverbs still in daily use.

Absence makes the heart grow fonder.

Actions speak louder than words.

All cats are grey in the dark.

All good things must come to an end.

All's fair in love and war.

All's well that ends well.

All that glitters is not gold.

All work and no play makes Jack a dull boy.

An apple a day keeps the doctor away.

Appearances can be deceptive.

Ask no questions and you'll be told no lies.

As well be hanged for a sheep as a lamb.

As you make your bed so must you lie on it.

As you sow, so shall you reap.

A bad workman always blames his tools.

A barking dog seldom bites.

Beauty is in the eye of the beholder.

Beggars can't be choosers.

Better late than never.

Better late than never but better never late.

Better safe than sorry.

A bird in the hand is worth two in the bush.

Birds of a feather flock together.

Blood is thicker than water.

Brevity is the soul of wit.

A burnt child dreads the fire.

Cast ne'er a clout till May be out.

A cat may look at a king.

Caveat emptor. (Latin) (Let the buyer beware.)

Charity begins at home.

Children should be seen but not heard.

Circumstances alter cases.

Cleanliness is next to godliness.

Clothes maketh not the man.

Comparisons are odious.

Constant dripping wears away the stone.

Cowards die many times before their death.

The creaking gate lasts longest.

Curiosity killed the cat.

Cut your coat according to your cloth.

Dead men tell no tales.

Deeds not words.

The devil finds work for idle hands to do.

Discretion is the better part of valour.

Do as I say, not as I do.

Do as you would be done by.

Don't change horses in midstream.

Don't count your chickens before they are hatched.

Don't cross the bridge until you come to it.

Don't cut off your nose to spite your face.

Don't throw out the baby with the bath water.

Don't hide your light under a bushel.

Don't kill the goose that lays the golden eggs.

Don't make a mountain out of a molehill.

Don't make a rod for your own back.

Don't meet trouble half-way.

Don't put all your eggs in one basket.

Don't put new wine into old bottles.

Don't put the cart before the horse.

Don't rob Peter to pay Paul.

Don't teach your grandmother to suck eggs.

Don't tell tales out of school.

A drowning man will clutch at a straw.

Ducks lay eggs; geese lay wagers.

The early bird catches the worm.

Early to bed, early to rise, makes a man healthy, wealthy and wise.

Easier said than done.

East, west, home's best.

Easy come; easy go.

Eavesdroppers never hear any good of themselves.
Empty vessels make the most sound.
The end justifies the means.
An Englishman's home is his castle.
Enough is as good as a feast.
Even a worm will turn.
Even the walls have ears.
Every cloud has a silver lining.
Every dog has his day.
Every little helps.
Everything comes to him who waits.
Example is better than precept.
Exchange is no robbery.

Faint heart ne'er won fair lady.
Familiarity breeds contempt.
Fine feathers make fine birds.
Fire is a good servant but a bad master.
First come, first served.
A fool and his money are soon parted.
Fools rush in where angels fear to tread.
Forbidden fruit tastes sweetest.
Forewarned is forearmed.
A friend in need is a friend indeed.

Gather ye rosebuds while ye may.
Give a dog a bad name and hang him.
Give a thief enough rope and he'll hang himself.
Give credit where it's due.
God helps those who help themselves.
God is on the side of the big battalions.
God tempers the wind to the shorn lamb.
Good fences make good neighbours.

Good wine needs no bush.

Great minds think alike.

Great oaks from little acorns grow.

Half a loaf is better than no bread.

Handsome is as handsome does.

Heaven helps those who help themselves.

He who hesitates is lost.

He who laughs last laughs longest.

He who pays the piper calls the tune.

He who touches pitch will be defiled.

Honesty is the best policy.

Honi soit qui mal y pense. (Old French) (Evil to him who evil thinks.)

Hunger is the best sauce.

A hungry man is an angry man.

If at first you don't succeed, try, try, and try again.

If something's worth doing, it's worth doing well.

If the cap fits, wear it.

If you want a thing done well, do it yourself.

Imitation is the sincerest form of flattery.

In for a penny, in for a pound.

In vino veritas. (Latin) (In wine there is truth.)

It never rains but it pours.

It's a long lane that has no turning.

It's an ill wind that blows nobody any good.

It's easy to be wise after the event.

It's never too late to mend.

It's no use crying over spilt milk.

It's no use spoiling the ship for a ha'porth of tar.

It's the last straw that breaks the camel's back.

It takes all sorts to make a world.

It takes two to make a quarrel.

Jack of all trades, master of none.

Judge not that ye be not judged.

The labourer is worthy of his hire.

Laugh and grow fat.

Laugh and the world laughs with you; weep and you weep alone.

Learn to walk before you run.

Least said, soonest mended.

Leave well alone.

Let not the pot call the kettle black.

Let not the sun go down on your anger.

Let sleeping dogs lie.

Let the cobbler stick to his last.

Like father, like son.

A little learning is a dangerous thing.

Little pitchers have long ears.

Little things please little minds.

Look after the pennies and the pounds will look after themselves.

Look before you leap.

Love laughs at locksmiths.

Make haste slowly.

Make hay while the sun shines.

A man is as old as he feels; a woman is as old as she looks.

Manners maketh man.

Many a little makes a mickle.

Many a mickle makes a muckle. (Scottish version)

Many hands make light work.

Marry in haste, repent at leisure.

Misfortunes never come singly.

A miss is as good as a mile.

Moderation in all things.

More haste, less speed.

The more you have, the more you want.

Nature abhors a vacuum.

Necessity is the mother of invention.

Never look a gift horse in the mouth.

Never trouble trouble till trouble troubles you.

New brooms sweep clean.

A nod is as good as a wink.

A nod is as good as a wink to a blind horse.

No man can serve two masters.

No names, no pack drill.

None but the brave deserve the fair.

No news is good news.

None so blind as those who will not see.

None so deaf as those who will not hear.

No pain, no gain.

No smoke without fire.

Nothing succeeds like success.

Nothing venture, nothing gain.

Once bitten, twice shy.

One good turn deserves another.

One man's meat is another man's poison.

One volunteer is worth two pressed men.

Opportunity seldom knocks twice.

Out of sight, out of mind.

Out of the frying pan into the fire.

Patience is a virtue.

The pen is mightier than the sword.

A penny saved is a penny gained.

Penny wise, pound foolish.

People who live in glass houses should not throw stones.

Per ardua ad astra. (Latin) (Through hardship to the stars.)

A pet lamb is a cross ram.

A place for everything and everything in its place.

Possession is nine tenths of the law.

Practice makes perfect.

Practise what you preach.

Prevention is better than cure.

Pride goes before a fall.

Procrastination is the thief of time.

The proof of the pudding is in the eating.

Punctuality is the politeness of kings.

The road to hell is paved with good intentions.

A rolling stone gathers no moss.

Sauce for the goose is sauce for the gander.

Self-praise is no recommendation.

Set a thief to catch a thief.

Silence gives consent.

Silence is golden.

A soft answer turneth away wrath.

Spare the rod and spoil the child.

Speak the truth and shame the devil.

Speech is silver, silence golden.

The spirit is willing, but the flesh is weak.

Still waters run deep.

A stitch in time saves nine.

The strength of a chain is in its weakest link.

Strike while the iron's hot.

Take care of the pennies and the pounds will take care of
themselves.

Tempus fugit. (Latin) (Time flies.)

There are plenty more fish in the sea.

There's many a good tune played on an old fiddle.

There's many a slip 'twixt the cup and the lip.

There's many a true word spoken in jest.

There's no smoke without fire.

A thing of beauty is a joy forever.

Those whom the gods love die young.

Time and tide wait for no man.

Time is money.

Time is the great healer.

Together we stand, divided we fall.

Too many cooks spoil the broth.

A trouble shared is a trouble halved.

Truth will out.

Two heads are better than one.

Two's company, three's a crowd.

Variety is the spice of life.

Verb. sap. (Latin abbreviated: *Verbum sat sapienti.*) (A word is enough for the wise.)

Virtue is its own reward.

Walls have ears.

Waste not, want not.

A watched pot never boils.

The way to a man's heart is through his stomach.

We never miss the water till the well runs dry.

What can't be cured must be endured.

Whatever's worth doing is worth doing well.

What the eye doesn't see, the heart doesn't grieve over.

When in doubt, do nowt.

When in Rome, do as the Romans do.

When one door shuts, another opens.

When the cat's away, the mice will play.

Where ignorance is bliss, 'tis folly to be wise.

Where there's a will, there's a way.

Where there's life, there's hope.

Where there's muck, there's money (or brass).

Why keep a dog and bark yourself?

A wild goose never laid a tame egg.

You can't burn the candle at both ends.

You can't get a quart into a pint pot.

You can't get blood out of a stone.

You can't have it both ways.

You can't have your cake and eat it.

You can't make an omelette without breaking eggs.

You can't make a silk purse out of a sow's ear.

You can't make bricks without straw.

You can't put an old head on young shoulders.

You can't run with the hare and hunt with the hounds.

You can't teach an old dog new tricks.

You have to make the best of a bad job.

You may lead a horse to water but you can't make him drink.

You scratch my back and I'll scratch yours.

TEST YOUR WORD POWER

Some proverbs seem to contradict each other, although each is true in certain circumstances. Complete the apparently contradictory proverbs.

1. He who hesitates is lost.

   _____ you leap.

2. Clothes maketh not the man.

   _____ fine birds.

3. Out of sight, out of mind.

   _____ grow fonder.

4. What's done can't be undone.

   _____ to mend.

5. Deeds not words.

    _____ I do.

Match up beginnings and endings with connecting lines.

6. When in doubt   think alike.

7. Dead men   please little minds.

8. Comparisons   sweep clean.

9. Still waters   die young.

10. Those whom the gods love   have long ears.

11. Fine words   run deep.

12. New brooms   are odious.

13. Great minds   butter no parsnips.

14. Little things   do nowt.

15. Little pitchers   tell no tales.

Supply the missing word in each proverb.

16. _____ is the better part of valour.

17. Even a _____ will turn.

18. Gather ye _____ while ye may.

19. Good wine needs no _____ .

20. A _____ man will clutch at a straw.

21. _____ is the spice of life.

22. Love laughs at _____ .

23. _____ makes the heart grow fonder.

24. You can't get _____ out of a stone.

25. _____ can't be choosers.

Find a proverb in the box with a meaning similar to each of the proverbs below.

Nothing venture, nothing gain.
First come, first served.
Every little helps.
Moderation in all things.
Once bitten, twice shy.
Appearances can be deceptive.
Deeds not words.
In for a penny, in for a pound.
Don't count your chickens before they are hatched.
One man's meat is another man's poison.

---

26. Enough is as good as a feast.

_____

27. As well be hanged for a sheep as a lamb.

_____

28. There's many a slip 'twixt the cup and the lip.

_____

29. A burnt child dreads the fire.

_____

30. All that glitters is not gold.

_____

31. The early bird catches the worm.

_____

32. Actions speak louder than words.

_____

33. Beauty is in the eye of the beholder.

_____

34. Many a little makes a mickle.

   _____

35. He who hesitates is lost.

   _____

Match up the proverbs in the box with the definitions that follow.

> Give a dog a bad name and hang him.
> The pen is mightier than the sword.
> When one door closes, another opens.
> A rolling stone gathers no moss.
> Empty vessels make the most sound.
> All's well that ends well.
> The creaking gate lasts longest.
> The proof of the pudding is in the eating.
> Good fences make good neighbours.
> Don't change horses mid-stream.
> Jack of all trades, master of none.
> Forewarned is forearmed.
> We never miss the water till the well runs dry.
> You scratch my back and I'll scratch yours.
> You may lead a horse to water but you can't make him drink.

36. If the final outcome is successful, all previous difficulties and disappointments are forgotten.

   _____

37. People in poor health all their lives often outlive their more robust friends and relations.

   _____

38. Ignorant people often do most of the talking.

   _____

39. If you know of a problem in advance, you can take appropriate steps.

   _____

40. However innocent a person may actually be, he is ruined forever if his reputation is destroyed.

_____

41. We need to respect the privacy of those close to us.

_____

42. It's better to do one thing really well rather than many things superficially.

_____

43. The written word is far more influential than physical force.

_____

44. You can't judge a project until it's completed.

_____

45. If you don't settle down and make a commitment, you won't achieve anything.

_____

46. We always take things for granted until we have to do without them.

_____

47. When one opportunity is taken away, another beckons.

_____

48. You praise me and I'll praise you.

_____

49. Choose the appropriate moment to make important changes.

_____

50. You can provide people with valuable opportunities but it's up to them to take advantage of them.

_____

Score:_____/50

Unit 12:
Prefixes

Dictionary definition:

Prefix: a syllable or syllables placed at the beginning of a word to make a new word

In this unit we focus on nearly 100 prefixes that in their turn give us the key to many thousands of words. Both your vocabulary and your spelling will benefit from isolating prefixes in this way and establishing exactly what their function is. Make sure you have a good dictionary by your side as you work through this unit.

NEGATIVE PREFIXES

Six prefixes can be used to make words negative:

a-, an- (Greek)	<u>a</u>moral, <u>a</u>theist, <u>a</u>nonymous
dis- (Latin)	<u>dis</u>advantage, <u>dis</u>appear, <u>dis</u>satisfied
in- (Latin) (il-, im-, ir-)	<u>in</u>capable, <u>in</u>visible, <u>il</u>legal, <u>im</u>possible, <u>ir</u>regular
mis- (Old French)	<u>mis</u>behave, <u>mis</u>diagnosis, <u>mis</u>spell
non- (Latin)	<u>non</u>-fiction, <u>non</u>sense, <u>non</u>-slip
un- (Old English)	<u>un</u>happy, <u>un</u>natural, <u>un</u>willing

▶ Note that if you join dis- or mis- to a word beginning with s-, you will have -ss-:
   dis + satisfied = dissatisfied
   mis + spell = misspell

▶ Note that if you join in- or un- to a word beginning with n-, you will have -nn-:
   in + numerable = innumerable
   un + natural = unnatural

▶ Note that in- changes before certain letters in the interest of euphony. It makes them far easier to say.

il- before l   i<u>l</u>legal
im- before m, p,   i<u>m</u>mature, i<u>m</u>possible
ir- before r   i<u>r</u>regular
  There is also the very irregular
  in + noble = i<u>g</u>noble

WARNING: Don't assume that a- and in- are always used in a
negative sense. See the Old English group of prefixes: abed, aground,
ashore (a- = in, on, to). See the Latin group of prefixes: invade,
intrude (in- = in, into).

TEST YOUR WORD POWER

Make these words opposite in meaning by adding an appropriate
negative prefix. Use your dictionary to help if you wish.

1.   _____   conditional

2.   _____   reputable

3.   _____   literate

4.   _____   patient

5.   _____   convenient

6.   _____   clear

7.   _____   responsible

8.   _____   sectarian

9.   _____   symmetrical

10.   _____   print

Explain the difference in meaning between the words in these pairs:

    disinterested and uninterested

11.   _____

12.   _____

    displace and misplace

13.   _____

14.   _____

disconnected and unconnected

15. _____

16. _____

distrust and mistrust

17. _____

18. _____

amoral and immoral

19. _____

20. _____

NUMBER PREFIXES

Words like one-sided, four-seater, eleven-plus are self-explanatory.
Where the prefixes come from Latin or Greek, however, it is not
always so clear.

uni-	(Latin)	one	unicellular, unicorn, unicycle, uniform, unite
mono-	(Greek)	one	monochrome, monocle, monocycle, monogamy, monolith, monologue, monopoly, monotonous
bi-	(Latin)	two	biannual, bicycle, biennial, bifocals, bigamy, bilingual, binoculars, biped, bisect
di-	(Greek)	two	dichotomy, dilemma, diphthong, diptych, duplicate
tri-	(Greek)	three	triangle, tricolour, tricycle, triplets, triplicate, tripod, triptych
quadr- quart-	(Latin)	four	quadrangle, quadrant, quadraphonics, quadrat, quadriplegic, quadruped, quadruple, quadruplets; quart, quarter, quartet, quartile, quarto

tetra-	(Greek)	four	tetrahedron, tetrameter, tetraplegic, tetrarch
quint-	(Latin)	five	quintet, quintile, quintuplets
penta-	(Greek)	five	pentagon, pentagram, pentameter, Pentateuch, pentathlon
ses-/sex-	(Latin)	six	sestet, sextennial, sextet, sextuplets
hex-	(Greek)	six	hexagon, hexameter, hexagram, hexahedron
sept-	(Latin)	seven	septet, septennial, septuagenarian, septuplets
hept-	(Greek)	seven	heptameter, heptahedron, Heptateuch, heptagon
oct-	(Greek & Latin)	eight	octagon, octahedron, octave, octet, octogenarian, octuplets, octopus
nona-	(Latin)	nine	nonagon, nonagenarian
dec-	(Latin)	ten	decade, decagon, decahedron, decimal
cent-	(Latin)	100	cent, centenarian, centenary, centimetre, centipede, century
mill-	(Latin)	1000	millennium, millibar, milligram, millimetre, millipede

TEST YOUR WORD POWER

True or false?

		True	False
21.	A <u>millipede</u> has a thousand legs.	☐	☐
22.	A <u>nonagenarian</u> is between 90 and 99 years old.	☐	☐
23.	A <u>unicycle</u> is the same as a <u>monocycle</u>.	☐	☐
24.	<u>Biannual</u> means the same as <u>biennial</u>.	☐	☐
25.	<u>Tetraplegia</u> is another term for <u>quadriplegia</u>.	☐	☐

Supply the words that best fit these definitions:

26. being able to speak two languages fluently   _____

27. eight children born at a birth   _____

28. the crime of marrying someone when you are already legally married to someone else   _____

29. the name given to the first five books of the Old Testament   _____

30. a six-sided figure (mathematics)   _____

SOME OLD ENGLISH PREFIXES

a- (on, in, to)	abed, about, above, adrift, afoot, alive, aloud, amid, ashore, astern
after- (after)	afterbirth, aftercare, afterlife, aftermath, afternoon, aftertaste, afterthought
be- (by)	bedazzle, bedeck, befriend, behead, bemoan, bespatter, bewilder
down- (downward)	downcast, downfall, downgrade, downtrodden
for- (prohibition)	forbid
(self-control)	forbear, forgo
(neglect)	forget, forsake
fore- (in front)	forebear, foreboding, forecast, forecourt, forefather, forehead, foresee, foretell
out- (away, from, beyond)	outcast, outdoors, outlandish, outlaw, outmanoeuvre, outstrip, outwit
through- ⎫ (through) thorough- ⎭	throughout, throughput; thoroughbred, thoroughfare, thoroughgoing
under- (beneath, below)	underage, undercover, underestimate, undernourished, understand, undertake, undervalue, underwear
up- (upwards)	update, upgrade, uphill, uplands, uproar, upturned
wel-/well- (well)	welcome, welfare; well-being, well-wisher

with- (against, back)   withdraw, withhold*, within, without, withstand

*Notice -hh-: with + hold = wit<u>hh</u>old

TEST YOUR WORD POWER

Which words from the list above best fit these definitions?

31. a feeling that something bad will happen   _____

32. to stand up against, to resist   _____

33. behind or towards the rear of a ship   _____

34. looking or sounding very odd and unfamiliar_____

35. looking downward (of eyes); sad, depressed _____

36. a main road through a town or village   _____

Give two meanings of 'aftermath'.

37. _____

38. _____

Explain the difference in meaning between forbear and forebear.

39. _____

40. _____

SOME LATIN PREFIXES

ab-, a- (away from)   abdicate, abnormal, abscond, absolve, abuse, avert

ad-* (towards)   accumulate, adhesive, adjoin, affect, aggregate, allot, announce, approach, arrive, assist, attract

ambi- (both)   ambidextrous, ambiguous, ambivalent,

ante- (before)   antecedent, antediluvian, antenatal, anteroom, anticipate

bene- (well)	benediction, benefactor, benefit, benevolent, benison
circum- (round)	circumcise, circumference, circumlocution, circumnavigate, circumstances
con-* (with)	cohere, collect, co-operate, combine, community, companion, compel, conference, congregation, connect, conspire, contagious, correct
counter- ⎫ (against) contra- ⎭	counter-attack, contraception, countermand, contraband, contradict, contravene
de- (down, from, of)	debar, deciduous, deduce, deport, descend, description, dethrone, detract
e-, ex- (out of)	eccentric, effect, emigrant, event, excavate, exhale, expel, export
extra- (beyond)	extra-curricular, extradite, extraordinary, extravagant, extrovert
in- (into)	immigrant, infectious, inhale, inscription, intrude, invade
inter- (between)	intercede, interchange, interject, intermediate, interrupt, interval
intra- (inside)	intramural, intrauterine, intravenous
intro- (to the inside)	introduce, introspection, introvert
multi- (many)	multicoloured, multimillionaire, multiple, multiply, multipurpose, multitude
ob- (against)	obdurate, obsolete, obstruct, obtrude, obviate, obvious, opponent
omni- (all)	omnipotent, omniscient, omnivorous
per- (through)	perambulate, perennial, permanent, permeable, perpetual, persecute
post- (after)	postgraduate, postmortem, postpone, postscript, post-war
pre- (before)	precocious, prejudge, prejudice, premature, prepare, prevent, pre-war
pro- (in place of, out, on behalf of)	proclaim, proconsul, progress, pronoun, propose, pro-slavery, provision

re- (again, back)	repay, repeat, reprint, retract, return, revise, rewrite
retro- (back)	retrograde, retrorocket, retrospect
se- (away from)	secede, secrete, sedate, seduce, segregate, select, separate
semi- (half)	semicircle, semicolon, semidarkness, semidetached, semi-final, semitone
sub-* (under)	subculture, subcutaneous, submarine, subordinate, subterranean, succumb, suffocate, suggest, summon, suppress, surreptitious
super- (above)	supercilious, superfluous, supernatural, supersede, supersonic, supervise
trans- (across)	transaction, transatlantic, transcribe, transfer, transfusion, translate, translucent, transparent, transport
ultra- (beyond)	ultra-fashionable, ultramarine, ultrasonic, ultrasound, ultraviolet

ad-, con-, sub-*

To make the new words easier to say, the final letter of these three prefixes sometimes changes. These changes are listed below so that you can be aware of what is happening. The prefixes still retain their meaning.

ad-   changes before c, f, g, l, n, p, q, r, s, t.
       accumulate, affect, aggregate, allot, announce, approach, acquire, arrive, assist, attract

con- changes before b, h, l, m, p, r, and some vowels.
       combine, cohere, collect, commit, companion, correct, cooperate

sub- changes before c, f, g, m, p, r.
       succumb, suffocate, suggest, summon, suppress, surreptitious

TEST YOUR WORD POWER

What is the meaning of these words?

41. subcutaneous _____

42. prejudice _____

43. ambidextrous _____

44. postmortem _____

45. omnipotent _____

46. ultramarine _____

47. intravenous _____

48. exhale _____

49. obdurate _____

50. surreptitious _____

Choose the definition that best fits each word.

51. ambivalent
(a) able to use either hand with ease ☐
(b) confusion over left and right ☐
(c) having mixed feelings ☐

52. circumlocution
(a) walking in circles ☐
(b) long-windedness ☐
(c) removing the kidneys ☐

53. benison
(a) victory ☐
(b) blessing ☐
(c) harvest ☐

54. supercilious
(a) vague ☐
(b) unnecessary ☐
(c) haughty ☐

55. benefactor
(a) someone who benefits from a will ☐
(b) someone who is making a good recovery ☐
(c) someone who gives money, help or support ☐

56. secede
    (a) withdraw formally from an alliance ☐
    (b) succeed ☐
    (c) postpone until the age of 21 ☐

57. antediluvian
    (a) ridiculously old-fashioned ☐
    (b) very much ahead of one's time ☐
    (c) unforgiving ☐

58. countermand
    (a) hold up at gunpoint ☐
    (b) revoke ☐
    (c) speak firmly ☐

59. omnivorous
    (a) very hungry ☐
    (b) widely read in a number of languages ☐
    (c) eating food of both plant and animal origin ☐

60. abscond
    (a) leave suddenly and secretly ☐
    (b) kidnap ☐
    (c) turn over a new leaf ☐

Explain clearly the difference in meaning between the words in these pairs.

contagious and infectious

61. _____

62. _____

extrovert and introvert

63. _____

64. _____

dethrone and abdicate

65. _____

66. _____

emigrant and immigrant

67. _____

68. _____

translucent and transparent

69. _____

70. _____

SOME GREEK PREFIXES

anti- (against)	antagonise, Antarctic, antibiotics, anti-clockwise, antidote, antifreeze, antipathy, antiseptic, antithesis, antonym
apo- (away from)	aphorism, apocalypse, apocrypha, apology, apostle, apostrophe
arch- (chief)	archangel, archbishop, arch-criminal, archetype, architect
auto- (self)	autism, autobiography, autocue, autograph, automatic, automaton
cata- (down, badly, against)	cataclysm, catalyst, cataract, catarrh, catastrophe, catatonic, catapult
dia- (through)	diabetes, diagnose, diagonal, diagram, dialogue, diameter, diaphanous, diorama
dys- (bad, difficult)	dysentery, dysfunction, dysgraphia, dyslexia, dyspepsia
em-, en- (within, inside)	embryo, empathy, emphasis; endemic, energise, energy
endo- (within)	endocardial, endocrine, endoderm, endoscope, endoskeleton
epi- (upon, in addition)	epidemic, epidermis, epigram, epigraph, epilepsy, epilogue, episode, epitaph, epithet, epitome
eu- (well)	Eucharist, eugenics, eulogy, euphemism, euphony, euphoria, euthanasia
hemi- (half)	hemiplegic, hemisphere
hetero- (other)	heterodox, heterogeneous, heterosexual
homo- (same)	homeopathy, homogenised, homonym, homophone, homosexual

hyper- (over, beyond)	hyperactive, hyperbole, hypercritical, hypermarket, hypersensitive, hypertension, hyperventilate
hypo- (under)	hyphen, hypo-allergenic, hypochondriac, hypocrisy, hypodermic, hypotension, hypotenuse, hypothermia
mega- (great)	megalith, megalomania, megaphone, megastar, megastore, megaton
meta- (across, after,with)	metabolism, metamorphosis, metaphor, metaphysical, method
micro- (small)	microbe, microchip, microcosm, microdot, microfilm, microscope
neo- (new)	neoclassical, Neolithic, neologism, neon, neonatal, neo-Nazi, neophyte, neoprene
ortho- (straight, right)	orthodontist, orthodox, orthography, orthopaedic, orthoptics
pan- (all)	panacea, pan-African, pancreas, pandemonium, panoply, panorama, pantechnicon, pantheism, pantomime
para- (beside)	parable, paragraph, parallel, paralyse, paramedic, paramilitary, paraplegic, parasite, parody
peri- (around, about)	perimeter, period, peripatetic, periphery, periscope, peritonitis
poly- (many)	polygamy, polyandry, polyanthus, polytechnic, polygamy, polyglot, polygon, polymath, Polynesia
pro- (before)	proboscis, prognosis, prologue, prophet, proscenium
proto- (first)	protagonist, protocol, protoplasm, prototype, protozoa
pseudo- (false)	pseudonym
syn- (with, together)	syllable, symmetry, sympathy, symphony, synagogue, synchronise, syndrome, synopsis
tele- (at a distance)	telecommunication, teleconferencing, telekinesis, telepathy, telephone, telescope, television

TEST YOUR WORD POWER

Give the meaning of these words.

71. diaphanous _____

72. telekinesis _____

73. pandemonium _____

74. megalomania _____

75. neonatal _____

76. panacea _____

77. polygyny _____

78. prototype _____

79. parable _____

80. panorama _____

Complete the words

81. a substance that kills germs   a_____

82. a name used by an author
     instead of his or her own   ps_____

83. words written about someone
     on his or her gravestone   e_____

84. a funny imitation of a serious
     piece of writing   p_____

85. a person who speaks a lot of
     languages   p_____

86. a device for viewing inside body
     cavities and organs   e_____

87. sudden outbreak of a disease or
     infection which affects large
     numbers of people   e_____

88. inability to write due to brain
     damage or disease   d_____

89.   the flexible elongated snout
of an elephant or tapir   p_____

90.   pleasantness of sound, especially
in pronunciation   e_____

True or false?

91.   An **antidote** counteracts the effects of poison. _____

92.   The **endoderm** is the last episode in a serial. _____

93.   A **neologism** is a newly coined word or
expression.   _____

94.   **Antipathy** is another word for sympathy.   _____

95.   A **polymath** is a mathematics lecturer.   _____

96.   The **Neolithic** period relates to the later part
of the Stone Age.   _____

97.   **Hypotension** is the opposite of hypertension. _____

98.   An **orthodontist** treats irregularities of the
eyes.   _____

99.   An **epigram** is a short witty saying.   _____

100. A **pantechnicon** is a technician.   _____

Score for Unit 12: _____/20

_____/10

_____/10

_____/30

_____/30

Total: _____/100

Unit 13:
Suffixes

Dictionary definition:

Suffix: a syllable or syllables placed at the end of a word to make a new word

DIMINUTIVES

The suffixes below once conveyed smallness, although frequently this sense has now been lost. Check the derivation of the words below in a good dictionary and you will see the part the suffixes play.

-cle (Latin)	article, corpuscle, cubicle, follicle, particle, pellicle, tabernacle, testicle
-een (Irish)	boreen, colleen, poteen
-en (Old English/ (Old French)	kitten, maiden
-ette, -et (French)	cigarette, coquette, kitchenette, maisonette, rosette; floret, islet, nymphet, pocket
-isk (Greek)	asterisk, basilisk, obelisk
-kin (Dutch)	bumpkin, cannikin, catkin, firkin, lambkin, manikin, napkin, pannikin, pipkin, siskin, spillikin
-let (French)	booklet, cutlet, driblet, droplet, flatlet, leaflet, piglet, rivulet, starlet, streamlet
-ling (Old English)	codling, darling, duckling, fledgling, gosling, nestling, sapling, sibling, suckling
-ock (Old English)	bullock, hillock
-ule (Latin)	capsule, globule, granule, module, nodule, pustule

TEST YOUR WORD POWER

Explain the derivation of these words and the part the suffix plays in each case.

1. pocket _____
2. asterisk _____
3. cutlet _____
4. nodule _____
5. testicle _____
6. corpuscle _____
7. poteen _____
8. firkin _____
9. coquette _____
10. darling _____

SOME ABSTRACT NOUN SUFFIXES

(Abstract nouns name ideas, concepts, emotions, qualities, states and conditions.)

-age (Latin)	bondage, courage, heritage, homage, leverage, verbiage, wreckage
-al (Latin)	betrayal, burial, denial, dismissal, portrayal, renewal, withdrawal
-ance (Latin)	abundance, alliance, annoyance, arrogance, endurance, resistance
-ence (Latin)	eminence, dependence, inference, persistence, prudence, somnolence
-dom (Old English)	boredom, freedom, martyrdom, officialdom, stardom, wisdom
-ery (Latin)	bravery, robbery, slavery, snobbery, treachery, trickery
-hood (Old English)	boyhood, childhood, neighbourhood, parenthood, priesthood, widowhood
-ice (Latin)	avarice, justice, malice, practice, service

-ion (Latin)	action, definition, devotion, ignition, intention, operation, preparation, sensation
-ism (Greek)	alcoholism, Catholicism, feminism, hedonism, patriotism, racism, socialism
-ity (Latin)	absurdity, complexity, hostility, humility, popularity, probity, simplicity, veracity
-ment (Latin)	achievement, astonishment, commitment, excitement, improvement, retirement
-ness (Old English)	fitness, forgiveness, happiness, gentleness, kindness, loneliness, weakness, weariness
-our/-or (Latin)	clamour, fervour, honour, labour; error, horror, pallor, terror, tremor
-ship (Old English)	citizenship, fellowship, friendship, hardship, leadership, membership, worship
-tude (Latin)	attitude, fortitude, gratitude, magnitude, servitude, solitude
-ty (Latin)	beauty, certainty, creativity, cruelty, honesty, royalty, safety
-ure (Latin)	closure, expenditure, exposure, failure, legislature, mixture, pleasure, seizure
-y (Latin/Greek)	consistency, decency, jealousy, orthodoxy

TEST YOUR WORD POWER

Use suffixes from the box to form abstract nouns from the words below. Use each suffix once only.

-age	-ism
-al	-ition
-ance	-ment
-ence	-our
-ion	-ure

Adding suffixes to base words is not always straightforward. Take care with any necessary spelling modifications. (Appendix A offers guidance on these modifications. Use a dictionary if you wish.)

11. interrupt _____

12. depart _____

13. punish _____

14. acquit _____

15. rely _____

16. drain _____

17. prefer _____

18. recognise _____

19. plagiarise _____

20. behave _____

Explain clearly the difference in meaning between the words in these pairs.

parentage and parenthood

21. _____

22. _____

barbarity and barbarism

23. _____

24. _____

populism and popularity

25. _____

26. _____

corruption and corruptibility

27. _____

28. _____

slavery and enslavement

29. _____

30. _____

Tick the correct spelling.

31. differance ☐
    difference ☐

32. perseverance ☐
    perseverence ☐

33. intelligance ☐
    intelligence ☐

34. adolescance ☐
    adolescence ☐

35. inheritance ☐
    inheritence ☐

36. correspondance ☐
    correspondence ☐

37. tolerance ☐
    tolerence ☐

38. conveniance ☐
    convenience ☐

39. appearance ☐
    appearence ☐

40. grievance ☐
    grievence ☐

SOME ADJECTIVE SUFFIXES

(Adjectives describe nouns and pronouns.)

-able (Latin)	capable, comfortable, manageable, miserable, noticeable, suitable, taxable, washable
-acious (Latin)	audacious, capacious, fallacious, loquacious, sagacious, tenacious, veracious, voracious
-al (Latin)	annual, comical, exceptional, infernal, pivotal, regal, royal, tidal, total

-an/-ane (Latin)	Cuban, human, pagan, sylvan, urban; humane, mundane, urbane
-ant/-ent (Latin)	arrogant, ignorant, pleasant, pregnant; fraudulent, innocent, persistent, violent
-ar (Latin)	lunar, molecular, peculiar, regular, secular, similar, singular
-arian (Latin)	antiquarian, humanitarian, sectarian, utilitarian
-arious (Latin)	gregarious, multifarious, vicarious
-ary (Latin)	contrary, exemplary, mercenary, primary, sedentary, stationary
-ate (Latin)	deliberate, desolate, fortunate, separate
-ent (See -ant.)	
-er (Old English)	better, dearer, harder, heavier, nicer, prettier, softer, tastier
-est (Old English)	best, dearest, hardest, heartiest, nicest, prettiest, softest, tastiest
-esque (French)	picaresque, picturesque, statuesque; Dantesque, Pinteresque
-ful (Old English)	boastful, careful, fretful, graceful, merciful, shameful, wasteful
-ible (Latin)	audible, defensible, edible, flexible, horrible, reversible, terrible
-ic/-ical (Latin/Greek)	angelic, bucolic, historic, rhythmic; cervical, metaphorical, pathological
-id (Latin)	candid, flaccid, horrid, morbid, placid, rabid, splendid, tepid, torpid
-ile (Latin)	agile, ductile, fragile, juvenile, mobile, prehensile, senile, tactile
-ive (Latin)	active, competitive, corrosive, expensive, passive, pensive
-le (Middle English)	brittle, fickle, gentle, humble, idle, nimble, supple
-less (Old English)	careless, fathomless, penniless, ruthless, senseless, skinless

-ly (Old English)	brotherly, ghastly, heavenly, hourly, lovely, quarterly, saintly
-oid (Greek)	asteroid, cuboid, hominoid, rhomboid, schizoid, spheroid, tabloid
-ory (Latin)	admonitory, auditory, compulsory, illusory, mandatory, sensory
-ose (Latin)	bellicose, comatose, grandiose, jocose, morose, otiose, verbose
-ous (Latin)	anxious, barbarous, courageous, dangerous, fabulous, mutinous
-some (English)	handsome, loathsome, tiresome, quarrelsome, wholesome
-ular (Latin)	angular, circular, granular, modular, molecular, muscular, pustular, tubular
-worthy (English)	creditworthy, newsworthy, noteworthy, roadworthy, seaworthy, trustworthy
-y (Old English)	angry, dirty, greedy, merry, muddy, sorry, sunny, witty

TEST YOUR WORD POWER

Give the meaning of these words.

41. audacious _____

42. sylvan _____

43. pensive _____

44. comatose _____

45. ruthless _____

Which words listed best fit these definitions?

46. able to think and judge wisely s_____

47. soft and limp f_____

48. capable of grasping by wrapping around p_____

49. typical of unsophisticated rural
     life   b_____

50. experiencing at second-hand
     through another person's
     thoughts and actions   v_____

Explain the difference in meaning between the words in each of
these pairs.

urban and urbane

51. _____

52. _____

regal and royal

53. _____

54. _____

human and humane

55. _____

56. _____

veracious and voracious

57. _____

58. _____

compulsory and mandatory

59. _____

60. _____

Complete these phrases by converting the nouns in brackets into
adjectives. Use a dictionary to help you if you wish.

61. a   _____   prayer (fervour)

62. a   _____   task (labour)

63. an   _____   answer (error)

64. a _____ accident (horror)

65. an _____ action (honour)

66. an _____ remark (intention)

67. _____ work (preparation)

68. a _____ story (sensation)

69. a _____ wave of the hand (dismissal)

70. a _____ attitude (snobbery)

Choose the definition that fits each word best.

71. tepid
    (a) unenthusiastic ☐
    (b) sinful ☐
    (c) lukewarm ☐

72. candid
    (a) frank ☐
    (b) synthetic ☐
    (c) suffocating ☐

73. otiose
    (a) loathsome ☐
    (b) pointless ☐
    (c) expensive ☐

74. loquacious
    (a) talkative ☐
    (b) pure ☐
    (c) translucent ☐

75. morose
    (a) close to death ☐
    (b) gloomy ☐
    (c) no longer manufactured ☐

76. gregarious
    (a) religious ☐
    (b) sociable ☐
    (c) miserly ☐

77. utilitarian
    (a) fundamental ☐
    (b) designed for practical use ☐
    (c) cheap and nasty ☐

78. arrogant
    (a) overbearing ☐
    (b) brutal ☐
    (c) extravagant ☐

79.	mundane	(a)	muddy	☐
		(b)	ordinary	☐
		(c)	worldly	☐
80.	tactile	(a)	concerning the sense of touch	☐
		(b)	tactful	☐
		(c)	constructive	☐

SOME VERB SUFFIXES

(Verbs are 'doing' and 'being' words.)

-ate (Latin)	advocate, anticipate, concentrate, defecate, eradicate, fascinate, implicate, obfuscate
-eer (Latin)	domineer, career, electioneer, profiteer, volunteer
-en (Old English)	blacken, broaden, darken, deepen, flatten, harden, lengthen, listen, loosen, open, soften, strengthen, sweeten
-er (Old English)	batter, flutter, glimmer, stagger, stutter, wander
-esce (Latin)	coalesce, convalesce, effervesce, deliquesce, effervesce, effloresce, phosphoresce
-fy (Latin)	amplify, beautify, deify, dignify, falsify, identify, magnify, notify, sanctify, satisfy, simplify, verify
-ise/-ize* (French/Greek)	baptise, compartmentalise, despise, devise, disguise, equalise, eulogise, finalise, minimise
-ish (English)	abolish, banish, cherish, establish, finish, nourish, perish, polish, punish, ravish
-le (English)	amble, babble, cuddle, giggle, gobble, mingle, smuggle, sparkle, struggle, wriggle

*The two suffixes -ise and -ize are alternative spellings for most verbs (Americans favour -ize). Some writers feel it's safer to use -ise because the *only* two-syllabled verb that has to end in -ize is 'capsize'. If, however, you prefer to use -ize, remember that there are at least 30 everyday verbs that must be spelt -ise (including advertise, exercise, supervise, surprise and televise).

TEST YOUR WORD POWER

Complete this table.

	Noun	Adjective	Verb
81.	criticism	critical	
82.	purity	pure	
83.	weakness	weak	
84.	gladness	glad	
85.	admonition	admonitory	

Give the meaning of these words.

86. deify   _____

87. eradicate   _____

88. coalesce   _____

89. supplicate   _____

90. venerate   _____

Add an appropriate suffix to these verbs.

91. hyphen_____

92. comprom_____

93. flour_____

94. quick_____

95. putre_____

Supply the words from the list of verb suffixes on page 153.

96. to recover one's health and strength
over a period of time after an illness   c_____

97. to praise highly in speech or in writing e_____

98. to shine faintly with a wavering light   g_____

99. to make obscure or unintelligible   o_____

100. to check that something is correct or
    true   v_____

Score for Unit 13: _____/10

                   _____/30

                   _____/40

                   _____/20

        Total _____/100

Unit 14:
Word Roots

Dictionary definition:

root: (language)
(i)   the source from which a word is formed
(ii)   the part of a word that is left when beginnings and endings
        are removed

Over the centuries, we have borrowed and adapted words from
many languages. In this Unit, we look closely at the Latin and Greek
sources of many of our modern English words.

Look at the two lists below. The first is derived from the Latin
for 'foot' and the second from the Greek word for 'time'. Notice
how much easier it is to understand the meaning of a word once
you have identified the root.

From Latin *pes*, *pedis* (foot, of the foot)

pedal	a lever operated by the foot
pedestal	the base (or foot) of a column
pedestrian	someone who travels on foot
pedicure	the care and treatment of the feet
pedometer	a device for measuring the distance travelled on foot
biped	an animal with two feet (such as man)
quadruped	a four-footed animal
sesquipedalianism	the practice of using unnecessarily long and cumbersome words (a foot and half in length, as it were!)

From Greek *khronos* (time)

chronic	lasting a long time (especially of an illness)
chronicle	a factual account of important events in the order in which they happened

<u>chron</u>ological	arranged in the order in which events happened (chronological order)
<u>chron</u>ometer	a device for measuring time exactly
<u>chron</u>ometry	the science of the accurate measuring of time
<u>chron</u>ostratigraphy	the branch of geology concerned with establishing the age of strata of rocks
ana<u>chron</u>ism	an error in chronology; setting a person, fashion, object, etc. in the wrong period (e.g. the clock striking in Shakespeare's *Julius Caesar*)
syn<u>chron</u>ise	to arrange for events to happen at the same time

These two lists are by no means exhaustive. You may well know other words that can be added and you will certainly discover more as time goes by. Consider, for instance, imp<u>ede</u> and imp<u>ed</u>iment. Anything that hinders or obstructs certainly gets 'under your feet' in one sense. See if you can find out the historical connection between the feet of a crane and the word p<u>ed</u>igree.

Studying word roots is fascinating and something that is easily possible with a good dictionary. (Look at the end of a dictionary entry for information about derivation.)

One hundred Latin and Greek roots will now be listed in three separate groups. Derivations will be given but not their meanings.

Use a dictionary to establish the exact meaning of any words that you are uncertain about and then answer the questions that follow.

Take your time. Don't necessarily aim to complete all the groups at one sitting. Enjoy exploring the connection between the present-day meaning and the meaning of the Latin or Greek root. This will help to 'fix' the word in the memory and is part of the process of 'making the word your own'.

GROUP A (LATIN NOUNS)

annus (year)	annual, annuity, anniversary, biennial, perennial, millennium
aqua (water)	aquamarine, aquarium, aquatic, aqueduct, aqueous

bellum (war)	bellicose, bellicosity, belligerent, belligerence
aput, capitis* (head)	cap, capital, capitation, captain, decapitate, recapitulate
corpus, corporis* (body)	corporate, corporeal, corps, corpse, corpulent, corpus
dens, dentis* (tooth)	dental, dentifrice, dentist, dentures, indenture
fides (faith)	confident, diffident, fideism, fidelity, fiducial
frater, fratis* (brother)	fraternal, fraternise, fraternity, fratricide
lex, legis* (law)	legal, legalise, legislate, legitimate, lexicon, privilege
luna (moon)	lunacy, lunar, lunate, lunatic
manus (hand)	amanuensis, manipulate, manual, manufacture, manuscript
mater, matris* (mother)	maternal, maternity, matriarch, matriarchy, matricide, matron
mors, mortis* (death)	mortal, mortality, mortgage, mortician, mortify, mortuary
pater, patris* (father)	paternal, paternity, patricide, patron, patronise, patronymic
rus, ruris* (countryside)	rural, rustic, rusticity, rusticate
urbs* (city)	suburb, suburban, urban, urbanise, urbane
verbum (word)	verb, verbal, verbalise, verbatim, verbiage, verbose
via (road)	via, viable, viaduct, viaticum
vir (man)	virago, virile, virility
vulnus, vulneris* (wound)	vulnerable, vulnerability, vulnerary

*The genitive form of the noun is given (e.g. caput = head, capitis = of the head) where this provides the root for some of the derivatives.

TEST YOUR WORD POWER

Which of the words in Group A best fit these definitions?

1.   obese _____

2.   crescent-shaped _____

3.   a morgue _____

4.   loyalty _____

5.   suave _____

6.   paste or powder for cleaning teeth _____

7.   a transparent bluish-green gemstone _____

8.   a society controlled by women _____

9.   a fixed sum paid on a yearly basis _____

10.   the murder of a brother _____

Choose the definition that fits each word best.

11.   A virago is   (a) a muscular man ☐
                 (b) an adolescent boy ☐
                 (c) an abusive woman ☐

12.   A patronymic is   (a) a surname ☐
                 (b) a bequest ☐
                 (c) a grandfather ☐

13.   An amanuensis is   (a) an elderly factory worker ☐
                 (b) an assistant who writes from
                 dictation ☐
                 (c) a glove maker ☐

14.   Verbatim means   (a) wordy ☐
                 (b) word for word ☐
                 (c) in a few words ☐

15.   Capitation means   (a) beheading ☐
                 (b) writing in capital letters ☐
                 (c) funding based on so much per
                 person ☐

Give the meaning of these words.

16. belligerent _____

17. legal _____

18. rustic _____

19. viable _____

20. vulnerable _____

Check your answers with the answers given at the back of the book.

GROUP B (LATIN VERBS)

Two forms of the Latin verbs are given in each case. The first is first person singular present tense, and the second is the past participle. Both forms can provide roots for derivatives.

ambulo, ambulatum (I walk) — amble, ambulance, ambulant, perambulate, perambulator (pram)

amo, amatum (I love) — amateur, amatory, amorist, amorous

audio, auditum (I hear) — audible, audience, audition, auditor, auditory, auditorium

caedo, caesum (I kill) — fratricide, germicide, infanticide, matricide, patricide, suicide

capio, captum (I seize) — capable, capacity, captivate, captive, captor, capture

cedo, cessum (I go) — precede, proceed, recede, succeed, success, succession

claudo, clausum (I close) — claustrophobia, cloister, exclude, include

credo, creditum (I believe) — accredited, credence, credible, credit, credulous, creed

curro (I run) — concur, courier, course, current, curriculum, cursive, cursor, cursory

dico, dictum (I say) — diction, dictionary, dictum, edict, indict, predict, prediction

duco, ductum (I lead) — abduct, conduct, deduce, ductile, introduce, seduce

erro, erratum (I wander)	aberrant, aberration, err, errant, erroneous, error
facio, factum (I do)	effect, efficient; fact, faction, factor, factotum, manufacture
fero, latum (I carry)	infer, prefer, refer, transfer; collate, collation, relate, translate
finio, finitum (I finish)	final, finalise, finality, finish; finite, infinite, infinity
fluo, fluxum (I flow)	affluent, effluent, fluent, influence; flux, influx
gradio, gressus (I walk)	egress,ingress, progress, progressive, regress, regression, regressive
habito, habitum (I inhabit)	cohabit, habitable, habitat, habitation, inhabit, inhabitant
haereo, haeresum (I stick)	adherent, adhesive, coherent, cohesive inherent
iacio, iactum (I throw)	ejaculate, eject, inject, object, project, reject
iungo, iunctum (I join)	conjugal, conjunction, joint, jointure, junction, juncture
lego, legatum (I send, I commission)	delegate, legacy, legate, legation, relegate relegation
lego, lectum (I choose) (I read)	elect, election, select, eligible lectern, lecture, legend, legible, dyslexic
loquor, locutus (I speak)	colloquial, elocution, eloquent, interlocutor, loquacious, soliloquy
mitto, missum (I send)	admit, emit, omit, remit, transmit; dismiss, emissary, missile, missionary, missive
monstro, monstratum (I show)	demonstrate, demonstration, monstrance remonstrate, remonstration
moveo, motum (I move)	mobile, mobilise, motion, motivate, motive, motor, move
oro, oratum (I speak)	oracle, oracular, oration, orator, oratory, peroration
pello, pulsum (I drive)	compel, impel, propel, repel, compulsory, impulsive, repulsive
pendeo (I hang)	impending, pendant, pending, pendulum, suspend, suspension

plico, plicatum (I fold)	complicate, complicity, explicit, implicate, implicit, imply, replicate
porto, portatum (I carry)	deport, export, import, transport, portable, porter, portfolio
puto, putatum (I think, I reckon)	compute, computer, impute, putative, repute, reputation
rego, rectum (I rule, I keep straight)	direct, rectify, rectitude, rector, regiment
rumpo, ruptum (I break)	disrupt, erupt, interrupt, rupture
scribo, scriptum (I write)	describe, inscribe, manuscript, prescribe, proscribe, scribble, scripture
seco, sectum (I divide)	bisect, dissect, insect, section
solvo, solutum (I solve, I loosen)	absolve, absolution, dissolute, dissolve, soluble, solution, solve
specto, spectatum (I look at)	aspect, inspect, respect, spectacle, spectacles, spectator
spero, speratum (I hope)	despair, desperado, desperate, desperation (i.e. having no hope)
tango, tactum (I touch)	contact, contiguous, contingent, tactile, tangent, tangible
tendo, tensum/tentum (I stretch)	extend, intend, tense, tensile, tension tent
teneo (I hold)	contain, continent, continual, continuous, retain, retentive, tenant
torqueo, tortum (I twist)	distort, retort, torque, tortuous, torture
traho, tractum (I drag)	attract, protract, retract, traction, tractor
venio, ventum (I come)	advent, adventure, convene, convent, convention, event
verto, versum (I turn)	avert, convert, pervert, revert; averse, converse, perverse, reverse
video, visum (I see)	evident, provide; revise, revision, visible, vision, visionary
vivo, victum (I live)	revive, revivify, victuals, vivacious, vivarium, vivid
voco, vocatum (I call)	advocate, evocative, provocative, provoke, vocabulary, vocation

TEST YOUR WORD POWER

Which of the words in Group B best fit these definitions?

21. the murder of a child less than a year
old   i_____

22. a sudden break of an organ or
membrane   r_____

23. a speech made in a play by a character
alone on the stage   s_____

24. a tall stand with a sloping top to hold
a reader's text or a speaker's notes   l_____

25. the concluding part of a speech
summing up the points made   p_____

26. gullible, too ready to believe   c_____

27. able to be heard   a_____

28. having more than enough money to
live on   a_____

29. to scrawl, to write hastily and untidily s_____

30. to divide something into two equal
parts   b_____

What is the meaning of these words?

31. amble   _____

32. desperado   _____

33. indict   _____

34. aberration   _____

35. ductile   _____

36. finite   _____

37. habitat   _____

38. tensile   _____

39. convene   _____

40. implicate   _____

Choose the definition that fits each word best.

41. recede
    - (a) come again ☐
    - (b) move back ☐
    - (c) accept grudgingly ☐

42. claustrophobia
    - (a) fear of spiders ☐
    - (b) fear of open spaces ☐
    - (c) fear of confined spaces ☐

43. factotum
    - (a) a boring person who knows everything ☐
    - (b) a factory worker ☐
    - (c) an employee who does all kinds of work ☐

44. infer
    - (a) to hint ☐
    - (b) to draw a conclusion ☐
    - (c) to start a fire ☐

45. tortuous
    - (a) full of twists and turns ☐
    - (b) painful ☐
    - (c) unbelievable ☐

46. revise
    - (a) to remember ☐
    - (b) to look at again ☐
    - (c) to lower the price ☐

47. evocative
    - (a) nostalgic ☐
    - (b) shouted loudly ☐
    - (c) able to bring a feeling vividly to mind ☐

48. portfolio
    - (a) a curriculum vitae (a CV) ☐
    - (b) a flat case for carrying papers ☐
    - (c) French windows ☐

49. tangible
    - (a) so tempting you feel you can taste it ☐
    - (b) so vivid you feel you can touch it ☐
    - (c) so noisy it hurts your eardrums ☐

50. spectacle
    - (a) a striking visual display ☐
    - (b) an old-fashioned monocle ☐
    - (c) reading glasses ☐

True or false?

		True	False
51.	An **amateur** is a person who takes part in a sport or pastime as a hobby and without being paid.	☐	☐
52.	To **captivate** is to take someone prisoner.	☐	☐
53.	**Ingress** is a form of indigestion.	☐	☐
54.	An **adherent** is a follower or supporter.	☐	☐
55.	**Continuous** means going on without a break.	☐	☐
56.	To **retract** means to withdraw or to take something back.	☐	☐
57.	To **avert** means to turn over.	☐	☐
58.	A **vivarium** is a structure in which animals are kept in semi-natural conditions for study, observation or as pets.	☐	☐
59.	To **emit** is to leave something out.	☐	☐
60.	To **rectify** is to put something right.	☐	☐

Give the meaning of the words in bold below.

61. a **cursory** check _____

62. a **soluble** aspirin _____

63. **conjugal** bliss _____

64. an **impulsive** action _____

65. the **putative** father _____

66. to **mobilise** an army _____

67. to **remonstrate** with someone _____

68. to **delegate** a task _____

69. to **project** your voice _____

70. to **suspend** judgment _____

Check your answers with the answers given at the back of the book.

GROUP C (GREEK)

anthrōpos (man)	anthropoid, anthropology, anthropocentric, anthropomorphic, misanthropist, philanthropist
biblion (book)	bibliographer, bibliography, bibliomancy, bibliomania, bibliophile
bios (life)	biography, biochemistry, biodiversity, biology, bionics
dēmos (people)	demagogue, democracy, demographics, demography, demotic
derma, dermat- (skin)	dermatitis, dermatologist, dermatology, epidermis, pachyderm
dunamis (power)	dynamic, dynamics, dynamism, dynamite, dynasty
ēlektron (amber)	electric, electricity, electrocute, electrolysis, electronics
erōs, erōt- (love)	erotic, erotica, eroticism, erogenous
gē (earth)	geocentric, geochemistry, geography, geology, geometry, geophysics
haima (blood)	anaemia, haemoglobin, haemophilia, haemorrhage, haemorrhoids
hudōr (water)	dehydrate, hydrocephalus, hydroelectric, hydrofoil, hydrophobia, hydroponics
hypnos (sleep)	hypnopaedia, hypnosis, hypnotherapy, hypnotic, hypnotist
hustera (womb)	hysteria, hysterical, hysterectomy
karkinos (crab)	cancer, cancerous, canker, carcinoma, carcinogenic
logos (word, reason)	biology, eulogy, catalogue, dialogue, logic, logical, logorrhoea, philology
metron (measure)	isometrics, meter, metre, metric, metrical, metronome, thermometer
morphē (form)	amorphous, anthropomorphic, morpheme,

	morphology
onoma (name)	acronym, anonymous, antonym, patronymic, pseudonym, homonym, synonym
pais, paid- (child, boy)	paediatrician, paediatrics, paedophile, pederast, pederasty
pathos (experience, suffering)	antipathy, apathy, empathy, pathology, pathos, psychopath, sympathy, telepathy
phobos (fear)	agoraphobia, arachnophobia, claustrophobia, hydrophobia, phobia, phobic
phōnē (sound, voice)	euphony, megaphone, microphone, phonetics, phonics, telephone
phōs, phōt (light)	photocopy, photogenic, photography, photon, photolysis, photosynthesis
polis (city)	acropolis, metropolis, metropolitan, politics, polity
psukhē (breath, soul, life)	psychedelic, psychiatry, psychic, psychology, psychopath, psychosis, psychosomatic
tekhnē (art, skill)	technical, technicality, technician, technique, technology
theos (god)	atheist, pantheist, theocracy, theology, theosophy
thermē (heat)	thermal, thermodynamics, thermometer, thermostat
trauma (wound)	trauma, traumatic, traumatise, traumatism
zōion (animal)	zoo, zoological, zoology

TEST YOUR WORD POWER

What is the meaning of these words?

71. acronym _____

72. logorrhoea _____

73. amorphous _____

74. paediatrician _____

75. hypnotherapy _____

True or false?

	True	False
76. An elephant is a **pachyderm**.	☐	☐
77. A **metronome** measures distances.	☐	☐
78. A **zoo** is a botanical garden.	☐	☐
79. The opposite of **philanthropist** is **misanthropist**.	☐	☐
80. A **bibliophile** dislikes books.	☐	☐

Explain the connection between the meaning of these words and the meaning of their Greek roots.

81. *biology* and *bios* (life)

_____

_____

82. *democracy* and *dēmos* (people)

_____

_____

83. *dynamic* and *dunamis* (power)

_____

_____

84. *erogenous* and *erōs* (love)

_____

_____

85. *technology* and *tekhnē* (skill)

_____

_____

Choose the definition that fits each word best.

86. metropolis   (a) an underground city   ☐
                           (b) an important city   ☐
                           (c) the capital city of a country   ☐

87. euphony
    (a) pleasing sound, especially in speech ☐
    (b) a musical instrument ☐
    (c) a tropical climbing plant ☐

88. psychedelic
    (a) unable to control powerful impulses ☐
    (b) relating to altered perceptions, as through the use of hallucinogenic drugs ☐
    (c) brain-dead but kept alive on a life-support machine ☐

89. pantheist
    (a) somebody who suffers from asthma ☐
    (b) a maker of underwear ☐
    (c) one who believe that God and nature are the same ☐

90. electrolysis
    (a) the removal of hair roots by electric currents ☐
    (b) the study of electricity ☐
    (c) torture by means of electrical impulses ☐

Explain the connection with these Greek roots.

91. What connection is there between a crab (*karkinos*) and cancer?

    _____

    _____

92. What is the connection between the womb (*hustera*) and hysteria?

    _____

    _____

93. What has amber (*ēlektron*) got to do with electricity?

    _____

    _____

94. Which two Greek words give us our English word hydrophobia?

_____

_____

95. Which two Greek words give us our English word thermometer?

_____

_____

Supply the missing words in these sentences.

96. _____ is the ability to understand, share and experience another person's feelings.

97. _____ is an emotional shock or hurt, which may have long-term effects on a person's behaviour or personality.

98. _____ is a hereditary disease, usually attacking only males, where the blood fails to clot sufficiently to stop excessive bleeding.

99. _____ is the scientific study of the earth's structure and physical processes, e.g. tides, earthquakes, gravitation and magnetism.

100. A _____ person always looks attractive in photographs.

Check your answers with the answers given at the back of the book.

Score for Unit 14:   _____/20

_____/50

_____/30

Total _____/100

Appendix A:
Some Spelling Rules When Adding Suffixes

Usually, it's a very straightforward matter adding a suffix to a base word:

certain + ty	=	certainty
govern + ment	=	government
drink + able	=	drinkable
accident + al + ly	=	accidentally
weight + less + ness	=	weightlessness

However, with four groups of base words, there are significant spelling changes when suffixes are added.

These changes are explained below. Bear in mind that vowel suffixes are those beginning with a, e, i, o, or u (y also counts as a vowel suffix) and consonant suffixes beginning with one of the other 20 letters of the alphabet.

Words ending in -e
▶ Keep -e when adding consonant suffixes:

taste + ful	=	tasteful
sincere + ly	=	sincerely

▶ Drop -e when adding a vowel suffix:

love + able	=	lovable
dine + ing	=	dining

Exceptions
▶ whilst, wisdom, truly, duly, ninth, argument, wholly, awful
▶ words like courageous, gorgeous, manageable, noticeable, where -e- keeps c or g soft so that they sound like s or j.

One-to-one words
This rule applies to all words of ONE syllable, ending in ONE consonant preceded by ONE vowel.

▶ No change when adding a consonant suffix:

fit + ness	=	fitness

sin + ful	=	sinful
glum + ly	=	glumly

▶ Double the final consonant before adding a vowel suffix:

fit + ing	=	fitting
sin + er	=	sinner
fun + y	=	funny

Exceptions

▶ Never double w, x or y. It would look very odd.

saw + ing	=	sawing
tax + ed	=	taxed

Two-one-one words

This rule applies to all words of TWO syllables, ending in ONE consonant preceded by ONE vowel.

▶ No change when adding a consonant suffix:

limit + less	=	limitless
regret + ful	=	regretful
allot + ment	=	allotment

▶ When adding a vowel suffix, say the word aloud. Which of the two syllables is stressed?

Stress on FIRST syllable, ONE consonant:

BUDget + ed	=	budgeted
LIMit + ing	=	limiting

Stress on SECOND syllable, TWO consonants:

forGET + ing	=	forgetting
forBID + en	=	forbidden

Exceptions

▶ Never double w, x or y. It would look very odd.

allow + ance	=	allowance
relax + ation	=	relaxation

▶ Three words always double their final consonant before a vowel suffix even though their first syllables are stressed.

kidnap + ed	=	kidnapped

outfit + er	=	outfitter
worship + ing	=	worshipping

▶ Take extra care with words ending in -l. They double before all vowel suffixes except -ity, -ise (or -ize).

cancel + ed	=	cancelled
quarrel + ing	=	quarrelling
but formal + ity	=	formality
legal + ise	=	legalise

▶ There are five tricky words where the stress changes and so sometimes you have to double the final consonant before a vowel suffix and sometimes you don't.

conFER	conFERRed	conFERRing	CONference
deFER	deFERRed	deFERRing	DEFerence
preFER	preFERRed	preFERRing	PREFerence
reFER	reFERRed	reFERRing	REFerence
transFER	transFERRed	transFERRing	TRANSference

Words ending in -y
Look at the letter immediately preceding the final -y.

▶ If the word ends in vowel + y, just add the vowel or consonant suffix:

enjoy + ing	=	enjoying
enjoy + ment	=	enjoyment

▶ If the word ends in consonant + y, change y to i before adding the suffix:

pretty + est	=	prettiest
beauty + ful	=	beautiful

Exceptions
▶ laid, paid, said; daily, gaily, gaiety, slain

▶ babyhood, dryness, shyness, slyness, wryness.

▶ Don't change y to i before a vowel suffix beginning with another i:

try + al	=	trial
try + ing	=	trying

Answers

DICTIONARY PRACTICE (UNIT I)

1. b
2. b
3. a
4. b
5. a
6. a
7. b
8. b
9. b
10. c
11. inventory
12. autobiography
13. soliloquy
14. ostentation
15. accolade
16. ecstasy
17. obituary
18. alliteration
19. inebriation
20. histrionics
21. The sentence should show that a **cynic** is someone who doubts everyone's goodness, sincerity or honesty.
22. The sentence should show that **disinterested** means having no selfish motives or not seeking personal gain. A disinterested person is motivated by concern for the welfare of others. It is not to be confused with 'uninterested' (bored).
23. The sentence should show that an **allusion** is a reference to something.
24. Note that **ironical** is not the same as 'sarcastic'. An ironical remark is a gently teasing remark which states the opposite of what is known to be the case. A sarcastic remark is meant to be hurtful.
25. To **infer** is to draw a conclusion. You could infer that it

was snowing if a visitor arrived with snow on his hair and shoulders. It does not mean to hint or suggest.

26. The sentence should show that **vehement** means showing strong or passionate feeling. One can make a vehement plea for a cause one cares deeply about.

27. The sentence should show clearly that **aggravate** means to make worse. It does not mean 'irritate'. A situation can be aggravated by a careless or tactless remark.

28. The sentence should not confuse **literally** and 'metaphorically'. If you say that you were literally glued to the television screen, you mean exactly this.

29. **Sceptical** means tending to doubt until convinced.

30. **Conscientious** means painstakingly careful. A conscientious student is always scrupulous about doing the very best he or she can at all times.

31. eccentric
32. diffident
33. denigrate
34. exonerate
35. exotic
36. aneurism/aneurysm
37. abrogate
38. eclectic
39. renege
40. avaricious
41. lintel
42. gable
43. dormer
44. architrave
45. joists
46. bargeboard
47. mullion
48. eaves
49. cornice
50. dado

THESAURUS AND DICTIONARY PRACTICE (UNIT 2)

1–5. (5 of these) flung, heaved, hurled, lobbed, pitched, shied, slung, tossed

6–10. (5 of these) erroneous concept, false notion, misapprehension, misconception, mistaken belief, misunderstanding

11–15. (5 of these) ecstatic, elated, overjoyed, radiant, rapturous, transported

16–20. (5 of these) candid, direct, frank, sincere, straightforward, truthful

21–25. (5 of these) disgraceful, highly improper, outrageous, reprehensible, shameful, shocking

26. swallow rapidly, choke

27. breathe quickly

28. breathe jerkily

29. breathe noisily

30. breathe with difficulty

31. respectful wonder mixed with fear

32. high regard

33. public show of respect and admiration

34. reverential devotion

35. respect

36. extremely funny, causing great amusement

37. silly, foolish, laughable

38. causing loud, boisterous laughter

39. using words and ideas in a clever, amusing way

40. funny/amusing

41. easily angered

42. easily annoyed

43. gloomily bad-tempered and spiteful

44. bad-tempered and spiteful

45. bad-tempered

46. payment for professional services

47. voluntary payment for professional services

48. regular monthly payment to an employee

49. regular weekly payment to an employee

50. payment for services rendered

51. A band is a group of musicians and vocalist(s) who play pop, jazz, rock or dance music.

52. An orchestra is a large group of musicians with a wide range of instruments (string, woodwind, brass and percussion) playing serious (usually classical) music.

53. A catalogue is a complete list of items for sale, display or reference.

54. A programme lists events and performers at a show, play or concert.
55. A pie is a sweet or savoury dish, baked in the oven, usually topped with a pastry crust.
56. A tart is a sweet dish with an under-layer of pastry but usually not with a top cover of pastry.
57. A casserole is a meat and vegetable dish cooked slowly in a covered container in the oven.
58. A stew is a meat and vegetable dish simmered in a saucepan on top of the stove.
59. An apron is a protective garment worn over the front of one's clothes, tied at the waist, with sometimes a bib attached.
60. A pinafore is a protective garment like a sleeveless dress worn over one's clothes when cooking, etc. It is usually full length.
61. infamous
62. forbid
63. showy
64. secret
65. beginner
66. remain
67. somnolent
68. refrain
69. fearless
70. stick
71. parsimonious
72. voracious
73. permanent
74. occasional
75. enthusiastic
76. retreat
77. joy
78. failure
79. wealth
80. release
81. succinct
82. precise
83. boastful
84. urban
85. discordant

86. compulsory
87. barren
88. guilty
89. frivolous
90. natural
91. lethargic – energetic
92. repellent – alluring
93. base – unadulterated
94. heedless – wary
95. callow – mature
96. ephemeral – lasting
97. renowned – obscure
98. naïve – sophisticated
99. manual – automatic
100. immaculate – filthy

PEOPLE (UNIT 3)

1. authoritarian – favouring strict discipline and subservience to authority
2. authoritative – commanding respect; trusted as being reliable
3. celibate – unmarried (perhaps through religious vows); abstaining from sex
4. chaste – sexually faithful; abstaining from sex on moral grounds
5. dominant – most important, most influential
6. domineering – asserting one's will over others; exercising excessive control over others
7. hypercritical – being excessively critical
8. hypocritical – seeming to have higher standards of morals than is in fact the case if the truth were known
9. sensual – appealing to the body (especially through food, drink, sex)
10. sensuous – appealing to the senses aesthetically (especially through music, poetry, art)
11. slender
12. brawny
13. cadaverous
14. rotund
15. petite

16. emaciated
17. buxom
18. obese
19. corpulent
20. gaunt
21. c
22. a
23. c
24. a
25. b
26. a
27. b
28. a
29. c
30. a
31. tranquil
32. frenetic
33. inconstant
34. loyal
35. famous (for good reasons)
36. notorious (for bad reasons)
37. rude
38. courteous
39. diligent
40. lazy
41. phlegmatic
42. sadistic
43. materialistic
44. sceptical
45. naïve
46. laconic
47. sarcastic
48. mercenary
49. misanthropic
50. lethargic

OCCUPATIONS (UNIT 4)

1. bees
2. irregularity in the teeth and jaw

3. soil management and crop production
4. lives of the saints
5. investigation of crimes scientifically
6. childhood diseases
7. compiling dictionaries
8. mental and emotional disorders
9. stuffing animals
10. x-rays
11. the human race
12. living things
13. the endocrine glands
14. the physical structure of the earth
15. the measurement of time
16. the weather
17. tumours
18. the eye
19. diseases
20. human society
21. caves
22. religion
23. poisons
24. animals
25. A councillor represents his or her ward on a local council.
26. A counsellor is trained to give guidance on personal problems.
27. An astrologer claims to analyse the effect of the stars and planets on human destiny.
28. An astronomer makes a scientific study of the stars and planets.
29. An entomologist studies insects.
30. An etymologist studies the origins of words.
31. gynaecologist
32. trichologist
33. mycologist
34. campanologist
35. psephologist
36. seismologist
37. graphologist
38. genealogist
39. philologist
40. dermatologist

41. theodolite
42. metronome
43. float
44. palette
45. baton
46. anvil
47. cleaver
48. chisel
49. gavel
50. forceps

SEXIST AND NON-SEXIST LANGUAGE (UNIT 5)

Reference only

ANIMALS, BIRDS AND INSECTS (UNIT 6)

1. horse
2. dog
3. cat
4. cow/ox
5. eagle
6. lupine
7. ursine
8. vulpine
9. asinine
10. saurian
11. leap
12. convocation
13. wedge
14. charm
15. watch
16. mules
17. swine
18. larks
19. mallard
20. rhinoceroses
21. codling
22. fry
23. joey

24. foal, colt or filly
25. cub, whelp
26. salmon
27. eel
28. hare
29. goat
30. swan
31. gander
32. jackass
33. stallion
34. drake
35. stag, buck
36. pen
37. queen
38. bitch, vixen, she-wolf
39. sow
40. ewe
41. cock
42. hen
43. buck
44. doe
45. bull
46. cow
47. form
48. lodge
49. holt
50. drey

CONFUSABLES (UNIT 7)

1. complimentary
2. dependants
3. counsellor
4. waive
5. voracious
6. equitable
7. contagious
8. exhaustive
9. economical
10. misplaced

11. deficient
12. invented
13. ingenious
14. fewer
15. masterly
16. implied
17. disinterested
18. libel
19. observation
20. historic
21. condensation
22. organisms
23. consistency
24. mural
25. ulcers
26. verge
27. strung
28. remedial
29. convulvulus
30. paediatrician
31. happening now; being in a place; a gift
32. to give formally
33. something that is refused, something that is substandard
34. to refuse to accept, to refuse to use
35. someone who is ill
36. not legally correct
37. opposite, reversed, contrary
38. to talk, to chat
39. a scheme, a plan, special piece of school work involving research
40. to throw (voice), to jut out, to show (film)
41. somebody one confides in
42. assured, not shy
43. to display something boldly or showily
44. to refuse to comply, to treat with contempt
45. more important than anything or anyone else
46. in effect the same as, amounting to, as good as
47. having more than one possible meaning
48. having conflicting feelings
49. (in literary criticism) a ludicrous descent from the elevated to the commonplace, an anti-climax

50.   the power or quality of evoking pity or sadness (especially in the arts)

EPONYMS (UNIT 8)

Reference only

AMERICANISMS (UNIT 9)

1.   chiropodist
2.   curriculum vitae, C.V.
3.   estate agent
4.   lodger
5.   nasty
6.   plain, ugly
7.   impudent
8.   angry
9.   scone
10.   crisps
11.   best mince, minced steak
12.   swede
13.   trousers
14.   underpants
15.   knickers
16.   vest
17.   draughts
18.   catapult
19.   see-saw
20.   noughts and crosses
21.   stroller
22.   baby carriage
23.   crib
24.   diaper
25.   sedan
26.   stick shift
27.   muffler
28.   gasoline, gas
29.   pantihose, pantyhose
30.   suspenders
31.   vest

32.   cuff
33.   truck farm
34.   parking lot
35.   trailer park
36.   truckstop
37.   crosswalk
38.   divided highway
39.   rotary, traffic circle
40.   sidewalk
41.   thumbtack
42.   billfold
43.   green onions
44.   faucet
45.   closet
46.   semi-detached house
47.   skirting board
48.   to grill
49.   beach hut
50.   eiderdown

FOREIGN WORDS AND PHRASES IN ENGLISH (UNIT 10)

1.   anno domini
2.   ante meridiem
3.   approximately
4.   curriculum vitae
5.   thanks be to God
6.   God willing
7.   example given
8.   and others
9.   et cetera
10.   ibid.
11.   that is
12.   nem. con.
13.   note carefully
14.   op. cit.
15.   per annum
16.   post meridiem
17.   p.p.
18.   post scriptum

19.   for the time being
20.   quod erat demonstrandum
21.   see
22.   Rest in peace.
23.   Please reply.
24.   seq.
25.   viz.
26.   emptor
27.   dictu
28.   nom
29.   faire
30.   tour
31.   a love letter
32.   a penetrating comment
33.   a remark with a double meaning
34.   a private conversation
35.   enjoyment of life
36.   self-possession
37.   something that helps you remember
38.   someone or something one particularly dislikes
39.   taking pleasure in the misery of others
40.   a romantic relationship
41.   folie de grandeur – delusions of greatness
42.   inamorata – a sweetheart
43.   lapsus linguae – a slip of the tongue
44.   doppelgänger – a double
45.   angst – uneasy, anxious foreboding
46.   guru – a spiritual leader
47.   embonpoint – plumpness
48.   bain-marie – a double saucepan
49.   bon mot – witticism
50.   fracas – a brawl

PROVERBS (UNIT 11)

1.   Look before (you leap).
2.   Fine feathers make (fine birds).
3.   Absence makes the heart (grow fonder).
4.   It's never too late (to mend).
5.   Do as I say not as (I do).

6.   When in doubt, do nowt.
7.   Dead men tell no tales.
8.   Comparisons are odious.
9.   Still waters run deep.
10.   Those whom the goods love die young.
11.   Fine words butter no parsnips.
12.   New brooms sweep clean.
13.   Great minds think alike.
14.   Little things please little minds.
15.   Little pitchers have long ears.
16.   Discretion
17.   worm
18.   rosebuds
19.   bush
20.   drowning
21.   Variety
22   locksmiths
23.   Absence
24   blood
25   Beggars
26.   Moderation in all things.
27.   In for a penny, in for a pound.
28.   Don't count your chickens before they're hatched.
29.   Once bitten, twice shy.
30.   Appearances can be deceptive.
31.   First come, first served.
32.   Deeds not words.
33.   One man's meat is another man's poison.
34.   Every little helps.
35.   Nothing venture, nothing gain.
36.   All's well that ends well.
37.   The creaking gate lasts longest.
38.   Empty vessels make the most sound.
39.   Forewarned is forearmed.
40.   Give a dog a bad name and hang him.
41.   Good fences make good neighbours.
42.   Jack of all trades, master of none.
43.   The pen is mightier than the sword.
44.   The proof of the pudding is in the eating.
45.   A rolling stone gathers no moss.
46.   We never miss the water until the well runs dry.

47.   When one door closes, another opens.
48.   You scratch my back and I'll scratch yours.
49.   Don't change horses mid-stream.
50.   You may lead a horse to water but you can't make him drink.

PREFIXES (UNIT 12)

1.   unconditional
2.   disreputable
3.   illiterate
4.   impatient
5.   inconvenient
6.   unclear
7.   irresponsible
8.   non-sectarian
9.   asymmetrical
10.   misprint
11.   disinterested – having no selfish motives
12.   uninterested – not interested, bored
13.   displace – move from usual position
14.   misplace – put in wrong place and so lose temporarily
15.   disconnected – the connection has been lost
16.   unconnected – there isn't a connection
17.   distrust – ⎫ Both mean regarding with suspicion, doubting
           ⎬ the honesty or probity of someone, but
18.   mistrust – ⎭ 'distrust' is stronger.
19.   amoral – not accepting that there are any moral standards to observe
20.   immoral – not conforming to accepted moral standards
21.   False (although this is what the word means)
22.   True
23.   True
24.   False
25.   True
26.   bilingual
27.   octuplets
28.   bigamy
29.   Pentateuch
30.   hexagon

31. foreboding
32. withstand
33. astern
34. outlandish
35. downcast
36. thoroughfare
37. consequences or after-effects
38. regrowth of grass after mowing
39. refrain (forbear)
40. ancestor (forebear)
41. under the skin
42. opinion held without good reason
43. able to use both hands equally well
44. medical examination of a dead person to establish cause of death
45. all-powerful
46. very bright blue
47. administered directly into a vein, existing in a vein
48. breathe out
49. stubbornly refusing to change opinion or course of action
50. kept secret (usually for fear of disapproval)
51. c
52. b
53. b
54. c
55. c
56. a
57. a
58. b
59. c
60. a
61. contagious – infection spread by touch
62. infectious – infection spread through the air
63. extrovert – more concerned with the outside world and social relationships than inner thoughts and feelings
64. introvert – more concerned with inner thoughts and feelings than with the outside world and social relationships
65. to dethrone – to remove a monarch from the throne, or an influential person from a position of power
66. to abdicate – to give up one's right to the throne or to give up one's responsibilities

67. emigrant – leaves to make a permanent home in a foreign country
68. immigrant – comes to live permanently in a foreign country
69. translucent – semi-transparent; light passes through but no distinct detail can be seen
70. transparent – light passes through and objects can be clearly seen on the other side
71. (especially of material) light, delicate and translucent
72. the ability to move objects at a distance by the power of the mind
73. wild and noisy confusion
74. delusion about one's power or importance
75. concerning new-born children
76. a cure for every trouble and illness
77. the custom or practice of having more than one wife at a time
78. the first or experimental product from which others are copied and developed
79. a simple story which illustrated a moral or a spiritual lesson
80. a view over a wide area
81. antiseptic
82. pseudonym
83. epitaph
84. parody
85. polyglot
86. endoscope
87. epidemic
88. dysgraphia
89. proboscis
90. euphony
91. True
92. False
93. True
94. False
95. False
96. True
97. True
98. False
99. True
100. False

SUFFIXES (UNIT 13)

1. little pouch (poke)
2. little star (aster)
3. little rib (costa)
4. little knot (nodus)
5. little witness (to virility) (testis)
6. small body (corpus)
7. little pot (of whiskey) (pota)
8. little fourth (vierde) – originally a quarter of a barrel
9. little cock (wanton) (coq)
10. little dear (deere)
11. interruption
12. departure
13. punishment
14. acquittal
15. reliance
16. drainage
17. preference
18. recognition
19. plagiarism
20. behaviour
21. parentage – lineage
22. parenthood – being a parent
23. barbarity – extreme cruelty or brutality
24. barbarism – state of being uncivilised and uncultured
25. populism – concern to represent or appear to represent the concerns of ordinary people
26. popularity – being generally liked and admired
27. corruption – depravity; loss of integrity and moral principles
28. corruptibility – the capability of being corrupted
29. slavery – the state of being a slave; the practice of owning slaves
30. enslavement – the loss of freedom of choice and action
31. difference
32. perseverance
33. intelligence
34. adolescence
35. inheritance
36. correspondence
37. tolerance

38.	convenience
39.	appearance
40.	grievance
41.	daring, recklessly bold
42.	full of woods and trees
43.	thoughtful and sad
44.	in a coma, torpid
45.	without pity or mercy
46.	sagacious
47.	flaccid
48.	prehensile
49.	bucolic
50.	vicarious
51.	urban – of a town or city
52.	urbane – sophisticated, elegant and refined
53.	regal – like a king or queen
54.	royal – of a king or queen or member of the royal family
55.	human – like a member of the human race
56.	humane – compassionate; inflicting the minimum of pain
57.	veracious – truthful
58.	voracious – having a huge appetite
59.	compulsory – must be done by rule or law
60.	mandatory – must be done by law (slightly stronger in sense)
61.	fervent
62.	laborious
63.	erroneous
64.	horrific/horrendous
65.	honourable
66.	intentional
67.	preparatory
68.	sensational
69.	dismissive
70.	snobbish
71.	c
72.	a
73.	b
74.	a
75.	b
76.	b
77.	b
78.	a

79. b
80. a
81. criticise (also -ize)
82. purify
83. weaken
84. gladden
85. admonish
86. to worship as a god
87. to destroy completely
88. to come together and form one mass
89. to beg earnestly for something
90. to revere, regard with great respect
91. hyphenate
92. compromise (not -ize)
93. flourish
94. quicken
95. putrefy
96. convalesce
97. eulogise (also -ize)
98. glimmer
99. obfuscate
100. verify

WORD ROOTS (UNIT 14)

1. corpulent
2. lunate
3. mortuary
4. fidelity
5. urbane
6. dentifrice
7. aquamarine
8. matriarchy
9. annuity
10. fratricide
11. c
12. a
13. b
14. b
15. c

16. aggressive
17. lawful
18. simple and rough
19. workable
20. capable of being hurt, damaged or attacked
21. infanticide
22. rupture
23. soliloquy
24. lectern
25. peroration
26. credulous
27. audible
28. affluent
29. scribble
30. bisect
31. to walk at a leisurely pace
32. a desperate and reckless person, especially a criminal
33. to charge someone formally with committing a crime
34. a totally uncharacteristic departure from normal behaviour
35. easily led, influenced or moulded
36. having an end or limit
37. place where an animal normally lives or a plant grows
38. able to be stretched
39. to cause people to come together (for a meeting)
40. to show or to suggest that someone is involved with something illegal or shameful
41. b
42. c
43. c
44. b
45. a
46. b
47. c
48. b
49. b
50. a
51. True
52. False
53. False
54. True
55. True

56. True
57. False
58. True
59. False
60. True
61. hasty and superficial
62. easily dissolved
63. married
64. done on the spur of the moment
65. assumed, supposed
66. organise, assemble and make ready
67. argue and express strong disapproval
68. pass to another
69. cause to be heard at a distance
70. delay temporarily
71. a word formed from the first letter or letters of several words
72. excessive talkativeness
73. having no definite form or shape
74. a specialist in children's development and diseases
75. the treatment of physical, mental and emotional diseases under hypnosis
76. True
77. False
78. False
79. True
80. False
81. Biology is the study of living things.
82. Democracy is a system by which the people elect their leaders.
83. Someone who is dynamic is energetic and forceful.
84. Erogenous means producing sexual excitement when stimulated.
    Erōs (love) means physical love.
85. Technology is the application of scientific knowledge for practical purposes. *Tekhnē* means skill.
86. b
87. a
88. b
89. c
90. a

91.   The ancient Greeks considered that the swollen veins around a cancerous tumour resembled the limbs of a crab.

92.   Hysteria was once thought to be specific to women and it was believed that hysteria originated in the uterus.

93.   Amber when rubbed produces electricity.

94.   The two Greek words *hudōs* and *phobos* give us the word hydrophobia.

95.   The two Greek words *thermē* and *metron* give us the word thermometer.

96   Empathy

97.   Trauma

98.   Haemophilia

99.   Geophysics

100.   photogenic